A YEAR OF MERCY WITH
POPE FRANCIS

Dec, 8, 2015- nov, 20, 2016

DAILY REFLECTIONS

A YEAR OF MERCY WITH
POPE FRANCIS

DAILY REFLECTIONS

Edited by Kevin Cotter

Our Sunday Visitor Publishing Division
Our Sunday Visitor
Huntington, Indiana 46750

Copyright © 2014 by Kevin Cotter. Published 2014

20 19 18 17 16 15   3 4 5 6 7 8 9

ISBN: 978-1-61278-835-7 (Inventory No. T1642)
eISBN: 978-1-61278-380-2
LCCN: 2014950435

Cover design: Tyler Ottinger
Cover art: Stefano Spaziani
Interior design: Sherri Hoffman

PRINTED IN THE UNITED STATES OF AMERICA

Table of Contents

Introduction

Jorge Bergoglio — now Pope Francis — had a fairly typical upbringing. He was a practicing Catholic and enjoyed many of the things that his peers enjoyed at the time: basketball, opera, classical Argentinian cinema, and tango. But when he was nearly seventeen he received a call that was far from ordinary — one that would change his life forever.

On the first day of spring he was on his way to meet up with his friends to celebrate Student Day, a national holiday in Argentina. When he passed his parish church, he suddenly felt the need to go to inside.

Upon entering, he noticed a priest there that he did not know and felt an indescribable urge to have the priest hear his confession. Following the confession, Jorge was overwhelmed by God's mercy and tenderness. This feeling of love and mercy, combined with the powerful sense of God's providence in bringing him to church and confession at this time, moved him deeply. He decided not to meet up with his friends and instead spent the rest of the day contemplating what had happened. It was then that he decided that he was called to the priesthood.

The day was September 21, the feast of St. Matthew. Recollecting the event, Pope Francis compared his encounter with the priest to St. Matthew's encounter with Jesus when Our Lord "looking upon him loved him, and said . . . 'follow me'" (Mk 10:21).

This definitive experience of mercy had a profound impact on Pope Francis, deeply influencing who he is. Mercy has become the theme of his entire papacy. It is his primary means for communicating the

Gospel to others, not just because of his personal experience, but also because of his conviction that it is through mercy that God wishes to reach all people. As he stated in a homily on March 17, 2013: "I think — and I say it with humility — that this is the Lord's most powerful message: mercy."

A Year of Mercy is all about helping you unpack this powerful message of mercy in your life.

This book is set up so that you can not only read the words of Pope Francis, but also reflect on their meaning for your life as you consider the questions that follow each meditation.

St. Francis de Sales, one of the great spiritual directors among the saints, was a master of prayer. He offered six steps to prayer that are still relevant today and will help you enter more deeply into meditation and conversation with the Lord.

1. **Place yourself in the presence of God.**

   Remember that God is near you. Take a moment to invite him into your time of prayer. Meet him as if you were meeting a friend.

2. **Ask God for his assistance.**

   Ask that he would help in your meditation. Pray that God uses this time to draw you closer to him.

3. **Read over a passage of Scripture or some other spiritual work.**

   In this case, your spiritual reading will be the words of Pope Francis, but also consider supplementing this with Scripture, the Catechism of the Catholic Church, or other spiritual readings.

4. **Take some time to reflect and think over what you have read.**

   Your goal is not to necessarily learn something, but to enter more deeply into a relationship with Jesus and to understand yourself and God more intimately. Listen to what God is trying to tell you.

5. **Have a conversation with God about your reflections and thoughts.**

   In this stage, you want to ask yourself: What stood out to you in your spiritual reading? What is God trying to tell you through what you just read? What feelings arise in your heart? Talk to God about these things.

6. **Conclude your time in prayer.**

   In your conclusion, St. Francis de Sales recommends thanking God for your time in prayer, making petitions for yourself and others, and developing a practical resolution. Take what insights you have gained and apply them to your life in a practical way. For example, do you need to be more faithful to prayer? Do you need to forgive someone?

As St. Francis de Sales and many other spiritual writers make clear: there is no perfect method or process for prayer, which is ultimately the work of the Holy Spirit. The reflections I've provided following the pope's words are only meant to serve as prompts toward prayer; use them when you find them helpful, but don't be afraid to allow the Spirit to move you wherever he wishes.

May Pope Francis' words lead all of us to a deep relationship with the mercy of God and a strong conviction that we must give this mercy to others.

With Hope in the Divine Will
Kevin Cotter
August 15, 2014
Feast of the Assumption of the Blessed Virgin Mary

Revolutionary Nature of Love

SOLEMNITY OF MARY THE MOTHER OF GOD

Whenever we look to Mary, we come to believe once again in the revolutionary nature of love and tenderness. In her we see that humility and tenderness are not virtues of the weak but of the strong who need not treat others poorly in order to feel important themselves. Contemplating Mary, we realize that she who praised God for "bringing down the mighty from their thrones" and "sending the rich away empty" (Lk 1:52-53) is also the one who brings a homely warmth to our pursuit of justice.

— *Evangelii Gaudium*

Reflection: Do you see yourself as the mighty or the lowly? Ask God to help you understand your true worth in light of his mercy — a sinner in need of grace and a cherished son or daughter of God.

Bruised, Hurting, and Dirty

I prefer a Church which is bruised, hurting, and dirty because it has been out on the streets, rather than a Church which is unhealthy from being confined and from clinging to its own security. I do not want a Church concerned with being at the center and which then ends by being caught up in a web of obsessions and procedures.

— *Evangelii Gaudium*

Reflection: What comes to mind as you read Pope Francis' words? How do you feel called to change your own heart, mind, or actions in light of them? What does God want you to do to help our Church become more merciful?

The Seven Corporal Works of Mercy

I would like to recall [the Seven Corporal Works of Mercy], because it will be good to hear them again: to feed the hungry; to give drink to the thirsty; to clothe the naked; to harbor the homeless; to visit the sick; to visit the imprisoned; to bury the dead. I encourage you to carry on your work with joy and to model it after Christ's, allowing all who suffer to encounter you and count on you in time of need.

— Address, June 14, 2014

Reflection: How familiar are you with the Seven Corporal Works of Mercy? How many have you practiced? Write or print out a list of the Seven Corporal Works of Mercy and place them on your refrigerator as a way to learn them and as a reminder to practice them.

Sinners in Need of Mercy

In the Mystery of the Incarnation of the Son of God there is also an aspect that is connected to human freedom, to the freedom of each one of us. Indeed, the Word of God pitched his tent among us, sinners who are in need of mercy. And we all must hasten to receive the grace that he offers us.

— Angelus, January 5, 2014

Reflection: Do you hasten to receive his grace? Do you really believe that you need it? So often we appear to want God's grace, but our lives don't reflect this desire. Do you meet him in prayer each day? Do you frequent the sacraments? What will you do to run to his mercy this week?

A New Heaven and a New Earth

God is God-with-us, God who loves us, God who walks with us.... Thus Christmas reveals to us the immense love that God has for humanity. From this too derives our enthusiasm, our hope as Christians, that in our poverty we may know that we are loved, that we have been visited, that we are accompanied by God; and we look upon the world and on history as a place in which we walk together with him ... toward a new heaven and a new earth.

— Angelus, January 5, 2014

Reflection: The Christmas season is a great time to reflect on life and to make new commitments. How will you walk with Christ this year to make our world a better place? Where can you spread God's mercy to make a difference?

Beauty Precedes Us

The new star that appears to the Magi was a sign of the birth of Christ. Had they not seen the star, these men would not have set out. The light goes before us, truth goes before us, beauty precedes us. God goes before us.

The prophet Isaiah said that God is like the flower of the almond tree. Why? Because in that region the almond is the first to flower. And God goes ever before, he is always the first to seek us, he takes the first step.

God goes ever before us. His grace precedes us and this grace appeared in Jesus. He is the Epiphany. He, Jesus Christ, is the manifestation of God's love. He is with us.

— Angelus, Epiphany, January 6, 2014

Reflection: Look back at what God has done in your life. When did you encounter him? Be grateful that he has gone before you, and have the courage to follow after him more closely.

Close to the Poor and Outcast

Our faith in Christ, who became poor, and was always close to the poor and the outcast, is the basis of our concern for the integral development of society's most neglected members. Each individual Christian and every community is called to be an instrument of God for the liberation and promotion of the poor, and for enabling them to be fully a part of society. This demands that we be docile and attentive to the cry of the poor and to come to their aid.

— *Evangelii Gaudium*

Reflection: Pope Francis is calling every Christian to help the poor. In what ways, do you currently show mercy to those in need? Ask the Lord for the grace to be docile and attentive to the needs of the poor and find practical ways to help them.

Don't Let Your Faith Be Extinguished

It is so important to keep this desire [for God] alive, this longing to behold the Lord and to experience him, to experience his love, to experience his mercy! If one ceases to thirst for the living God, faith is in danger of becoming a habit, it risks being extinguished, like a fire that is not fed. It risks becoming "rancid," meaningless.

— Address, Meeting with Catechumens, November 23, 2013

Reflection: When in your life have you experienced the Lord's love and mercy the most? In times of suffering? In times of joy? In times of sin? Remember the times when the Lord was close to you. Find opportunities to encounter the Lord's mercy. Pray that it would give greater meaning and purpose to your relationship with him.

The Smell of the Sheep

An evangelizing community gets involved by word and deed in people's daily lives; it bridges distances, it is willing to abase itself if necessary, and it embraces human life, touching the suffering flesh of Christ in others.

Evangelizers thus take on the "smell of the sheep" and the sheep are willing to hear their voice. An evangelizing community is also supportive, standing by people at every step of the way, no matter how difficult or lengthy this may prove to be. It is familiar with patient expectation and apostolic endurance.

— *Evangelii Gaudium*

Reflection: Is there someone in your life who needs to know that you are standing by him or her every step of the way? Who needs a phone call, a kind note, or a visit? Make time for a small act of mercy.

1/22/16 (Fri) - I asked Elaine + D
to go to N. Shore LIJ to see Rosemary
Ryan Early - pulmonary fibrosis -
hospice.

A City on a Hill

We Christians must do this: replace malice with innocence, replace power with love, replace pride with humility, replace status with service.

Being disciples of the Lamb means not living like a "besieged citadel," but like a city placed on a hill, open, welcoming, and supportive. It means not assuming closed attitudes but rather proposing the Gospel to everyone, bearing witness by our lives that following Jesus makes us freer and more joyous.

— Angelus, January 19, 2014

Reflection: How can you replace malice with innocence, power with love, pride with humility, and status with service in your life? How could these acts of mercy make you freer and more joyous?

Three Essential Words

Please, thank you, sorry. Three essential words!

We say please so as not to be forceful in family life: "May I please do this? Would you be happy if I did this?" We do this with a language that seeks agreement.

We say thank you, thank you for love! But be honest with me, how many times do you say thank you to your wife, and you to your husband? How many days go by without uttering this word, thanks!

And the last word: sorry. We all make mistakes, and on occasion someone gets offended in the marriage, in the family, and sometimes — I say — plates are smashed, harsh words are spoken, but please listen to my advice: don't ever let the sun set without reconciling. Peace is made each day in the family: "Please forgive me," and then you start over.

— Address, Pilgrimage of Families, October 26, 2013

Reflection: The psalmist says, "Set a guard over my mouth, O Lord, keep watch over the door of my lips" (141:3). With our words we can quickly spread frustration and anger or mercy and love. Where have you failed with your words? To whom do you need to say, please, thank you, and sorry more often?

He Forgives Us Forever

When the Father beholds the wounds of Jesus he forgives us forever, not because we are good, but because Jesus paid for us. Beholding the wounds of Jesus, the Father becomes most merciful.

This is the great work of Jesus today in heaven: showing the Father the price of forgiveness, his wounds. This is the beauty that urges us not to be afraid to ask forgiveness; the Father always pardons, because he sees the wounds of Jesus, he sees our sin, and he forgives it.

— *Regina Caeli*, June 1, 2014

Reflection: Do you have a hard time forgiving yourself for past faults? God doesn't. He wants to forgive you, and forgive you forever. Be open to God's mercy to help you move on from the past. The beauty of mercy is that it truly makes us new.

Open Our Cold Hearts

We need to implore his grace daily, asking him to open our cold hearts and shake up our lukewarm and superficial existence....

How good it is to stand before a crucifix, or on our knees before the Blessed Sacrament, and simply to be in his presence! How much good it does us when he once more touches our lives and impels us to share his new life!

— *Evangelii Gaudium*

Reflection: The Chaplet of Divine Mercy has a beautiful prayer: "Eternal God, in whom mercy is endless and the treasury of compassion inexhaustible, look kindly upon us and increase your mercy in us, that in difficult moments we might not despair nor become despondent, but with great confidence submit ourselves to your holy will, which is Love and Mercy itself." Pray this prayer. Thank God for his mercy. Ask him to help you understand his plan for how you are to share it with others.

The Greatest Treasure of All

What gives us true freedom, true salvation, and true happiness is the compassion, tenderness, and solidarity of his love. Christ's poverty, which enriches us, is his taking flesh and bearing our weaknesses and sins as an expression of God's infinite mercy to us.

Christ's poverty is the greatest treasure of all: Jesus' wealth is that of his boundless confidence in God the Father, his constant trust, his desire always and only to do the Father's will and give glory to him.

— Lenten Message 2014

Reflection: Our real riches are found in our trust in God. Take some time to evaluate where your level of trust is with him. Fully entrust yourself to him once more, or even for the first time.

Too Many Words

We have at our disposal so much information and so many statistics on poverty and human tribulations. There is a risk of being highly informed bystanders and disembodied from these realities, or to have nice discussions that end up in verbal solutions and disengagement from the real problems.

Too many words, too many words, too many words, and nothing is done!... What's needed is work, Christian testimony, going to the suffering, getting close to them as Jesus did.

— Address, June 14, 2014

Reflection: Do you currently practice a corporal work of mercy on a regular basis? Find a way to help someone in need consistently, no matter how small your effort might be. Be part of the solution, and be a witness of God's mercy to change the world.

What Should the Church Strip Herself of?

But I would, as a pastor, ask myself as well: What should the Church strip herself of?

She must strip away every kind of worldly spirit, which is a temptation for everyone; strip away every action that is not for God, that is not from God; strip away the fear of opening the doors and going out to encounter all, especially the poorest of the poor, the needy, the remote, without waiting. Certainly not to get lost in the shipwreck of the world, but to bear with courage the light of Christ, the light of the Gospel, even in the darkness, where one can't see, where one might stumble.

She must strip away the seeming assurance structures give, which, though certainly necessary and important, should never obscure the one true strength it carries within: God.

— Address, October 4, 2013

Reflection: What is God asking you to strip away from your life? Where is he asking you to be a light in the midst of darkness? To be merciful instead of self-centered?

Sourpusses

One of the more serious temptations which stifles boldness and zeal is a defeatism which turns us into querulous and disillusioned pessimists, "sourpusses." Nobody can go off to battle unless he is fully convinced of victory beforehand. If we start without confidence, we have already lost half the battle, and we bury our talents.

While painfully aware of our own frailties, we have to march on without giving in, keeping in mind what the Lord said to St. Paul: "My grace is sufficient for you, for my power is made perfect in weakness" (2 Cor 12:9).

— *Evangelii Gaudium*

Reflection: Where do you lack confidence? When do you bury your talents? Ask God for the boldness to share his mercy with others.

The Revolution of Tenderness

The Gospel tells us constantly to run the risk of a face-to-face encounter with others, with their physical presence which challenges us, with their pain and their pleas, with their joy which infects us in our close and continuous interaction.

True faith in the incarnate Son of God is inseparable from self-giving, from membership in the community, from service, from reconciliation with others. The Son of God, by becoming flesh, summoned us to the revolution of tenderness.

— *Evangelii Gaudium*

Reflection: How have you experienced Christ's tenderness? Where is he calling you to live out a revolution of tenderness and mercy? In your family? In your parish? In your workplace? Take time to contemplate God's love for you, and then ask the Lord who he is calling you to love this week.

Do This Unfailingly Each Day

I invite all Christians, everywhere, at this very moment, to a renewed personal encounter with Jesus Christ, or at least an openness to letting him encounter them; I ask all of you to do this unfailingly each day. No one should think that this invitation is not meant for him or her.

— *Evangelii Gaudium*

Reflection: How can we give mercy if we have not encountered the mercy of Jesus Christ? Are you willing to renew this encounter, or even be open to it? If so, commit to opening yourself to the Lord each day in your prayer time. You might even use the simple prayer of St. Faustina — "Jesus, I trust in you, Jesus, I trust in you, Jesus, I trust in you."

So Many Difficulties, Problems, Dark Moments

But in what sense is the Church holy if we see that the historical Church, on her long journey through the centuries, has had so many difficulties, problems, dark moments? How can a Church consisting of human beings, of sinners, be holy? Sinful men, sinful women, sinful priests, sinful sisters, sinful bishops, sinful cardinals, a sinful pope? Everyone. How can such a Church be holy? . . .

Christ loved the Church, by giving himself on the cross. And this means that the Church is holy because she comes from God who is holy; he is faithful to her and does not abandon her to the power of death and of evil (cf. Mt 16:18).

— General Audience, October 2, 2013

Reflection: How does knowing that Christ loved the Church despite all of our weaknesses and failings change the way you love the Church despite its weaknesses today?

Not a News Item

How can it be that it is not a news item when an elderly homeless person dies of exposure, but it is news when the stock market loses two points? This is a case of exclusion.

Can we continue to stand by when food is thrown away while people are starving? This is a case of inequality.

Today, everything comes under the laws of competition and the survival of the fittest, where the powerful feed upon the powerless. As a consequence, masses of people find themselves excluded and marginalized: without work, without possibilities, without any means of escape.

— *Evangelii Gaudium*

Reflection: We can practice mercy through our thoughts and simple actions. See if you can go an entire week without wasting any food. Think of those who go without as you make sacrifices to not waste any of your food.

The Most Innocent Among Us

Among the vulnerable for whom the Church wishes to care with particular love and concern are unborn children, the most defenseless and innocent among us.... The Church cannot be expected to change her position on this question....

It is also true that we have done little to adequately accompany women in very difficult situations, where abortion appears as a quick solution to their profound anguish, especially when the life developing within them is the result of rape or a situation of extreme poverty. Who can remain unmoved before such painful situations?

— *Evangelii Gaudium*

Reflection: The Church's position on abortion is a beautiful stand for human life from its earliest stages. But we must also help women who are in crisis pregnancies. Do you have a pro-life crisis pregnancy center in your area? Ask them what they need and spread the word in your parish.

Find the Door Open

In the Church, the God we encounter is not a merciless judge, but like the father in the Gospel parable. You may be like the son who left home, who sank to the depths, farthest from the Gospel. When you have the strength to say: I want to come home, you will find the door open. God will come to meet you because he is always waiting for you, God is always waiting for you, God embraces you, kisses you, and celebrates.

That is how the Lord is, that is how the tenderness of our heavenly Father is.

— General Audience, October 2, 2013

Reflection: Read the story of the Merciful Father in Luke 15:11-32. Imagine yourself as the Prodigal Son. What is God calling you to do?

A Field Hospital

Today, we can think of the Church as a "field hospital." Excuse me, but I repeat it, because this is how I see it, how I feel it is: a "field hospital." Wounds need to be treated, so many wounds! So many wounds! There are so many people who are wounded by material problems, by scandals, also in the Church.... People wounded by the world's illusions....

Mercy first means treating the wounds. When someone is wounded, he needs this immediately, not tests, such as the level of cholesterol and one's glycemic index.... Specialized treatments can be done, but first we need to treat the open wounds.

I think this is what is most important at this time. And there are also hidden wounds, because there are people who distance themselves in order to avoid showing their wounds closer.

— Address, March 6, 2014

Reflection: What wounds do you see around you? Who is hurting and has distanced themselves from you or others? What can you do to respond to them with mercy immediately?

I Can Do All Things

FEAST OF THE CONVERSION OF ST. PAUL

We need to be strong every day of our lives, to carry forward our life, our family, our faith. The apostle Paul said something that will benefit us to hear: "I can do all things in him who strengthens me" (Phil 4:13). When we face daily life, when difficulties arise, let us remember this: "I can do all things in him who strengthens me."

The Lord always strengthens us; he never lets strength lack. The Lord does not try us beyond our possibilities. He is always with us.

— General Audience, May 14, 2014

Reflection: Fortitude gives us the courage to carry on in difficult circumstances. In what area of your life do you need God's strength right now? Give this area up to God in prayer and continue to have hope that he will give you the strength.

It Is Better for Him Not to Go to Mass!

If any one of us does not feel in need of the mercy of God, does not see himself as a sinner, it is better for him not to go to Mass! We go to Mass because we are sinners and we want to receive God's pardon, to participate in the redemption of Jesus, in his forgiveness.

— General Audience, February 12, 2014

Reflection: What motivates you to go to Mass? Do you view yourself as a sinner in need of grace? A righteous person doing his duty? Examine your motives and ask Jesus to continue to change your heart and mind so that you recognize your need for his mercy.

What Weighs You Down?

In this Gospel passage [of the Samaritan woman] we likewise find the impetus to "leave behind our water jar," the symbol of everything that is seemingly important, but loses all its value before the "love of God." We all have one, or more than one!

I ask you, and myself: "What is your interior water jar, the one that weighs you down, that distances you from God?" Let us set it aside a little and with our hearts; let us hear the voice of Jesus offering us another kind of water, another water that brings us close to the Lord.

— Angelus, March 23, 2014

Reflection: We are filled with so many things. Take time to be filled with the mercy of God. He will bring you freedom from anxiety, from resentments, from selfishness. What weighs you down? What distances you from God? Allow the mercy of God to be the number one priority in your life.

The Greatest of the Virtues

[Saint Thomas Aquinas] explains that, as far as external works are concerned, mercy is the greatest of all the virtues: "In itself mercy is the greatest of the virtues, since all the others revolve around it and, more than this, it makes up for their deficiencies."

— *Evangelii Gaudium*

Reflection: The First Letter of Peter tells us, "Above all hold unfailing your love for one another, since love covers a multitude of sins" (4:8). We can all think of the many deficiencies that we have that hold us back in our relationships with God and others. Respond to others with love and mercy as a way to overcome these.

Misericordia

"*Misericordia*" [mercy], [is] a Latin word meaning ... to "give the heart to the wretched," those in need, those who are suffering. That is what Jesus did: he opened his heart to the wretchedness of man. The Gospel has a wealth of episodes which present the *misericordia* of Jesus, his love freely given for the suffering and the weak.

— Address, June 14, 2014

Reflection: Think about when Jesus extends his mercy to those in the Gospel. The lepers. The blind. The paralytics. The good thief on the cross. He not only gives them healing, he gives them his love. Lord Jesus, make us like you. Help us to give mercy with love.

The Greatest Sinners

To encounter Jesus also means allowing oneself to be gazed upon by him. "But, Father, you know," one of you might say to me, "you know that this journey is horrible for me, I am such a sinner, I have committed many sins ... how can I encounter Jesus?"

And you know that the people whom Jesus most sought out were the greatest sinners ... the people — those who believed themselves righteous — would say: this is no true prophet, look what lovely company he keeps! He was with sinners....

And he said: I came for those in need of salvation, in need of healing.

— Homily, December 1, 2013

Reflection: Do you consider yourself righteous or a sinner? When asked who he was, Pope Francis' first response was: "I am a sinner." How do you see yourself? What does this say about your response to God's mercy?

To Give One's Life

Jesus says something remarkable to us: "Greater love has no man than this, that a man lay down his life for his friends." Love always takes this path: to give one's life. To live life as a gift, a gift to be given — not a treasure to be stored away.

— Homily, *Domus Sanctae Marthae*, May 14, 2013

Reflection: What kind of friend are you? Are you willing to lay down your life for your friends? Do you show them small acts of kindness and mercy? Who can you reach out to today?

If You Are With an Atheist

If you happen to be with an atheist who tells you that he does not believe in God, you can read him the whole library, where it says that God exists, and where it is proven that God exists, and he will not believe. [However,] if in the presence of this same atheist you witness to a consistent, Christian life, something will begin to work in his heart.... It will be your witness that brings him the restlessness on which the Holy Spirit works.

— Homily, *Domus Sanctae Marthae*, February 27, 2014

Reflection: What role does mercy play in your witness? Are you merciful to those around you at work or in the marketplace? Do you act in such a way that makes others restless about the joy within you?

Look at My Son, Jesus

Mary is blessed for her faith in God, for her faith, because her heart's gaze was always fixed on God.... Mary says to us:

Look at my son, Jesus, keep your gaze fixed on him, listen to him, speak with him. He is gazing at you with love. Do not be afraid! He will teach you to follow him and to bear witness to him in all that you do, whether great and small, in your family life, at work, at times of celebration. He will teach you to go out of yourself and to look upon others with love, as he did.

— Message, October 12, 2013

Reflection: Mary, Mother of Jesus, we turn to you. Teach us how to look upon your merciful son and to speak with him. Help us to learn how to bear witness to him and to love like him. Hail Mary ...

The Only Light

Loving others is a spiritual force drawing us to union with God; indeed, one who does not love others "walks in the darkness" (1 Jn 2:11), "remains in death" (1 Jn 3:14), and "does not know God" (1 Jn 4:8).

[Pope] Benedict XVI has said that "closing our eyes to our neighbor also blinds us to God," and that love is, in the end, the only light which "can always illuminate a world grown dim and give us the courage needed to keep living and working."

— *Evangelii Gaudium*

Reflection: Sometimes other people can be a source of frustration. We tell ourselves: They don't get it. They aren't faithful. They're living life in the wrong way. In the end, we are called to recognize the wrong, but also to love God by loving them. Choose mercy over judgment.

Privileged Recipients

If the whole Church takes up [the] missionary impulse, she has to go forth to everyone without exception. But to whom should she go first? When we read the Gospel we find a clear indication: not so much our friends and wealthy neighbors, but above all the poor and the sick, those who are usually despised and overlooked, "those who cannot repay you" (Lk 14:14).

— *Evangelii Gaudium*

Reflection: The poor and outcast are often the last people on our minds. Ask the Lord to change your heart and mind to think of the poor. God calls us to look to them first.

The Lord Is With Us

Jesus remains present and active in the affairs of human history through the power and the gifts of his Spirit; he is beside each of us: Even if we do not see him with our eyes, he is there! He accompanies us, he guides us, he takes us by the hand, and he lifts us up when we fall down.

The risen Jesus is close to persecuted and discriminated Christians; he is close to every man and woman who suffers. He is close to us all.... The Lord is with us! Do you believe this? Then let's say it together: the Lord is with us!

— *Regina Caeli*, June 1, 2014

Reflection: Do you lose sight of God in your sufferings, or do you draw near to him? This week try to pray in moments of distress. Reach out to him in small ways when you are challenged or feel weak. He is there to help you.

Fills Us With Passion

[A] relationship with the Lord is not intended as a duty or an imposition. It is a bond that comes from within. It is a relationship lived with the heart: it is our friendship with God, granted to us by Jesus, a friendship that changes our life and fills us with passion, with joy.

— General Audience, June 4, 2014

Reflection: Is your relationship with God filled with passion and joy? Or is it filled with guilt, obligation, duty, or indifference? Consider how to deepen your relationship with God. Start by contemplating his mercy. He has so much love for you.

Are We Tuned Into God?

We need to be receiving antennas that are tuned into the Word of God, in order to become broadcasting antennas! One receives and transmits. It is the Spirit of God who makes the Scriptures come alive, who makes us understand them deeply and in accord with their authentic and full meaning! ...

What place does the Word of God have in my life, in my everyday life? Am I tuned into God, or into the many buzzwords, or into myself? This is a question that every one of us needs to ask him or herself.

— Address, October 4, 2013

Reflection: What place does the Word of God have in your life? If we are going to transmit the Gospel and the mercy of God to others, we must be receiving that mercy each day. Read Matthew 14:6-21 and observe Jesus' care for the suffering. Ask the Lord to let you experience his heart and love for others.

An Intense Desire

The primary reason for evangelizing is the love of Jesus which we have received, the experience of salvation which urges us to ever greater love of him. What kind of love would not feel the need to speak of the beloved, to point him out, to make him known? If we do not feel an intense desire to share this love, we need to pray insistently that he will once more touch our hearts.

— *Evangelii Gaudium*

Reflection: Do you have an intense desire to share God's love? If not, is this because you haven't experienced his love deeply enough yourself? Find a retreat center in your area where you can enkindle the love of God more powerfully in your life.

Fill Your Heart With Faces and Names!

Every human being is the object of God's infinite tenderness, and he himself is present in their lives. Jesus offered his precious blood on the cross for that person. Appearances notwithstanding, every person is immensely holy and deserves our love. Consequently, if I can help at least one person to have a better life, that already justifies the offering of my life.

It is a wonderful thing to be God's faithful people. We achieve fulfillment when we break down walls and our heart is filled with faces and names!

— *Evangelii Gaudium*

Reflection: Our lives are amazing gifts, especially when we give them to others. Think about one small but merciful action you can make today that could brighten someone's day. Fill your heart with faces and names!

The Compassion of Jesus

We must have the heart of Jesus, who, "when he saw the crowds, he had compassion for them, because they were harassed and helpless, like sheep without a shepherd" (Mt 9:36). Seeing the crowds, he feels compassion for them. I like to dream of a Church who lives the compassion of Jesus.

Compassion is to "suffer with," to feel what the others feel, to accompany them emotionally.

— Address, June 16, 2014

Reflection: We are often so caught up in our own comfort, problems, or desires that we fail to see others and have compassion on them. Lord, give us your heart. Help us suffer with those around us. Fill our hearts with more love.

Forgive, and You Will Be Forgiven

"Be merciful, just as your Father is merciful. Do not judge, and you will not be judged; do not condemn, and you will not be condemned. Forgive, and you will be forgiven; give, and it will be given to you.... For the measure you give will be the measure you get back" (Lk 6:36-38).

What these passages make clear is the absolute priority of "going forth from ourselves towards our brothers and sisters" as one of the two great commandments which ground every moral norm and as the clearest sign for discerning spiritual growth in response to God's completely free gift.

— *Evangelii Gaudium*

Reflection: St. Faustina said: "He who knows how to forgive prepares for himself many graces from God. As often as I look upon the cross, so often will I forgive with all my heart." Who needs your forgiveness? Let Jesus' death on the cross help you make this step.

God's Logic

Jesus reasons with God's logic, which is that of sharing. How many times we turn away so as not to see our brothers in need! And this looking away is a polite way to say, with white gloves, "Sort it out for yourselves." And this is not Jesus' way: this is selfishness. Had he sent away the crowds, many people would have been left with nothing to eat. Instead those few loaves and fish, shared and blessed by God, were enough for everyone.

And pay heed! It isn't magic, it's a "sign": a sign that calls for faith in God, provident Father, who does not let us go without "our daily bread," if we know how to share it as brothers.

— Angelus, August 3, 2014

Reflection: When it comes to sharing, do we think with God's logic or our own? Do we remain indifferent, or are we obedient to God's call to engage with those in need? How can you share you time, talent, and resources with those around you this week?

Spiritual Worldliness Kills!

To this world it doesn't matter that there are children dying of hunger; it doesn't matter if many families have nothing to eat, do not have the dignity of bringing bread home; it doesn't matter that many people are forced to flee slavery, hunger and flee in search of freedom. . . .

It is unthinkable that a Christian — a true Christian — be it a priest, a sister, a bishop, a cardinal or a pope, would want to go down this path of worldliness, which is a homicidal attitude. Spiritual worldliness kills! It kills the soul! It kills the person! It kills the Church!

— Address, October 4, 2013

Reflection: What do you think Pope Francis means by spiritual worldliness? How does our own lack of caring and mercy kill our souls? Ask the Lord to make you more sensitive to the needs of others, especially the poor.

The Law of Love

Valentine's Day

Let us ask the Lord to help us understand the law of love. How good it is to have this law! How much good it does us to love one another, in spite of everything. Yes, in spite of everything! St. Paul's exhortation is directed to each of us: "Do not be overcome by evil, but overcome evil with good" (Rom 12:21). And again: "Let us not grow weary in doing what is right" (Gal 6:9).

— *Evangelii Gaudium*

Reflection: What is the law of love? Loving even when it hurts. Doing what is right even when no one is looking. In God's mercy, he's done all of these things for us. He had taught us a new way, and now it is our turn to do this for others.

Lord, Have Mercy on Me a Sinner

I would like to recall [a] parable, another one of Jesus' stories, when he spoke about one of these Pharisees who was standing in ... the Temple saying [in effect]: "Lord, I thank you that I am not like the other men. I do everything I'm supposed to do. I'm perfect."

Jesus tells us that there was a sinner — a publican ... in back of the Temple.... The publicans were considered to be traitors to their people because they collected taxes on behalf of the Roman Empire. But the only thing this man — this publican — said over and over again was, "Lord, have mercy on me a sinner!"

Referring to the publican, Jesus says this man was justified — was pardoned — rather than the other.

— Homily on the Forty-third Anniversary of the Community of Sant'Egidio, September 24, 2011, *Only Love Can Save Us*

Reflection: The Pharisee had pride; the tax collector had humility. By choosing humility over pride, we allow God's mercy to work powerfully in our life. The litany of humility is a great way to build up this virtue. Search for it online and pray it each day this week.

Who Is This Innkeeper?

There is a biblical icon that expresses, in all its depths, the mystery that shines through the anointing of the sick: it is the parable of the Good Samaritan contained in the Gospel of Luke (10:30-35).... The parable says that the Good Samaritan takes care of the suffering man by pouring oil and wine on his wounds.... Finally, the suffering person is entrusted to an innkeeper, so that he might continue to care for him, sparing no expense.

Now, who is this innkeeper? It is the Church, the Christian community — it is us — to whom each day the Lord entrusts those who are afflicted in body and spirit, so that we might lavish all of his mercy and salvation upon them without measure.

— General Audience, February 26, 2014

Reflection: Read the parable of the Good Samaritan in Luke 10:25-37. Imagine yourself as the innkeeper in the story. How can you practice the corporal work of mercy of visiting the sick?

In the Household

Relationships based on faithful love, until death, like marriage, fatherhood, being child or sibling, are learned and lived in the household. When these relationships form the basic fabric of a human society, they lend cohesion and consistency.

It is therefore not possible to be part of a people, to feel as a neighbor, to take care of someone who is more distant and unfortunate if, in the heart of man, these fundamental relationships, which give him security in openness toward others, are broken.

— Message to the First Latin American Congress
of Pastoral Care of the Family, August 6, 2014

Reflection: Our family relationships help us learn the virtue of mercy as we develop the habits of loving, forgiving, and serving one another. Where is God calling you to grow in mercy within your family? Where is it difficult to love right now? Ask God for the strength to increase your love.

The Lazy Addiction to Evil

Ash Wednesday marks the beginning of the Lenten journey of forty days, which will lead us to the Easter Triduum, the memorial of the Lord's passion, death, and resurrection, and the heart of the mystery of our salvation. Lent prepares us for this most important moment; therefore, it is a "powerful" season, a turning point that can foster change and conversion in each of us.

We all need to improve, to change for the better. Lent helps us and thus we leave behind old habits and the lazy addiction to the evil that deceives and ensnares us.

— General Audience, March 5, 2014

Reflection: What are you doing for Lent this year? How will it help you leave behind your old habits and lazy addictions? How will it lead you to become more merciful?

Why Must We Return to God?

The exhortation which the Lord addresses to us through the prophet Joel is strong and clear: "Return to me with all your heart" (Joel 2:12). Why must we return to God? Because something is not right in us, not right in society, in the Church, and we need to change, to give it a new direction. And this is called needing to convert!

Once again Lent comes to make its prophetic appeal, to remind us that it is possible to create something new within ourselves and around us, simply because God is faithful, always faithful, for he cannot deny himself, he continues to be rich in goodness and mercy, and he is always ready to forgive and start afresh. With this filial confidence, let us set out on the journey!

— Homily, March 5, 2014

Reflection: What's not right with you at the moment? Do you want to return to God with all of your heart in this area? Do you trust that he can create something new in your life?

Source of Living Water

In some places a spiritual "desertification" has evidently come about, as the result of attempts by some societies to build without God or to eliminate their Christian roots.... In these situations we are called to be living sources of water from which others can drink. At times, this becomes a heavy cross, but it was from the cross, from his pierced side, that Our Lord gave himself to us as a source of living water. Let us not allow ourselves to be robbed of hope!

— *Evangelii Gaudium*

Reflection: How does God's mercy fill you up to be a living source of water? Take time this week to be filled. Where are the deserts around you? Take time this week to be a source of hope.

Go to Mass Like Sinners

The "Confession" which we make at the beginning [of Mass] is not "pro forma," it is a real act of repentance! I am a sinner and I confess it, this is how the Mass begins! We should never forget that the Last Supper of Jesus took place "on the night he was betrayed" (1 Cor 11:23). In the bread and in the wine which we offer and around which we gather, the gift of Christ's body and blood is renewed every time for the remission of our sins. We must go to Mass humbly, like sinners, and the Lord reconciles us.

— General Audience, February 12, 2014

Reflection: The Mass is a deep encounter with the mercy of the Lord. Next time you are there, try to use each element of the Mass to meditate on his mercy. What is he saying to you through the prayers, the readings, and the Eucharist?

Always Capable of Transforming Us

Feast of the Chair of St. Peter

Simon denied Jesus in a dramatic moment of the Passion; Saul harshly persecuted the Christians. But they both welcomed God's love and allowed themselves to be transformed by his mercy; they thus became friends and apostles of Christ. This is why they continue to speak to the Church, and still today they show us the way to salvation.

And should we perchance fall into the most serious sins and the darkest of nights, God is always capable of transforming us too, the way he transformed Peter and Paul; transforming the heart and forgiving us for everything, thus transforming the darkness of our sin into a dawn of light.

— Angelus, June 29, 2014

Reflection: The Bible is filled with characters like Sts. Peter and Paul who committed the most serious sins. What can you learn about God's mercy amidst their grave mistakes? What does this tell you about your own faults, no matter how small or large they may be?

Jesus' Love

Jesus' love is great, Jesus' love is merciful, Jesus' love forgives; but you have to open yourself, and to open oneself means to repent, to accuse oneself of the things that are not good and which we have done. The Lord Jesus gave himself, and he continues to give himself to us, in order to fill us with all of the mercy and grace of the Father.

— General Audience, December 11, 2013

Reflection: Are you open to God's mercy? The Lord gives himself to us, but are we willing to give ourselves to him? What do you still need to give over to him?

Christ's Love Is Different

By making himself poor, Jesus did not seek poverty for its own sake but, as St. Paul says, "that by his poverty you might become rich." This is no mere play on words or a catchphrase. Rather, it sums up God's logic, the logic of love, the logic of the Incarnation and the Cross.

God did not let our salvation drop down from heaven, like someone who gives alms from their abundance out of a sense of altruism and piety. Christ's love is different!... He did it to be among people who need forgiveness, among us sinners, and to take upon himself the burden of our sins. In this way he chose to comfort us, to save us, to free us from our misery.

— Lenten Message 2014

Reflection: Jesus chose to give our salvation not as a gift from afar, but to save us by being among us. This Lent, how can you do the same? Where can you serve others in person rather than just giving from a distance?

The Weight of Our Sin

The grace of the sacraments nourishes in us a strong and joyful faith, a faith that knows how to stand in wonder before the "marvels" of God and how to resist the idols of the world.... It is important, when we feel the weight of our sin, to approach the Sacrament of Reconciliation.

— General Audience, November 6, 2013

Reflection: Do we hold other things to be more important than the sacraments? Is our pride more important than receiving the Sacrament of Penance? Is our selfishness with our time more important than our attendance at Mass? What idols do we seek instead of God's mercy in the sacraments?

The Renunciation of St. Francis

The renunciation of St. Francis tells us simply what the Gospel teaches: following Jesus means putting him in first place, stripping ourselves of the many things that we possess that suffocate our hearts, renouncing ourselves, taking up the cross, and carrying it with Jesus. Stripping ourselves of prideful ego and detaching ourselves from the desire to possess, from money, which is an idol that possesses.

— Address, October 4, 2013

Reflection: Is Jesus in first place in your life right now? What suffocates your heart right at this moment? What's one small thing you can give up this week to make room to experience more of God's mercy?

What Will My Cross Be Like?

There is no fruitful apostolic work without the Cross.... [We] might think: "What will happen to me? What will my cross be like?" We do not know, but there will be a cross, and we need to ask for the grace not to flee when it comes. Of course it scares us, but this is precisely where following Jesus takes us.

Jesus' words to Peter come to mind: "Do you love me? Feed ... Do you love me? Tend ... Do you love me? Feed ..." (cf. Jn 21:15-19), and these were among his last words to him: "They will carry you where you do not wish to go." He was announcing the Cross.

— Homily, *Domus Sanctae Marthae*, September 28, 2013

Reflection: In life, we all have a cross to carry — weaknesses, and battles that we face. In these moments, we have a choice. We can choose to carry our crosses or let them drag us around instead. What have you been doing with your cross lately? Turn to Jesus to help you. God's mercy is waiting for you.

Sacrificing Christians

The pain and the shame we feel at the sins of some members of the Church, and at our own, must never make us forget how many Christians are giving their lives in love. They help so many people to be healed or to die in peace in makeshift hospitals. They are present to those enslaved by different addictions in the poorest places on earth. They devote themselves to the education of children and young people. They take care of the elderly who have been forgotten by everyone else. They look for ways to communicate values in hostile environments. They are dedicated in many other ways to showing an immense love for humanity inspired by the God who became man.

— *Evangelii Gaudium*

Reflection: Do you know people who practice sacrificial mercy toward others? How can you show them gratitude? How can you follow their example?

Pours Upon Us All of His Mercy

The Eucharistic celebration is much more than simple banquet: it is exactly the memorial of Jesus' paschal sacrifice, the mystery at the center of salvation. "Memorial" does not simply mean a remembrance, a mere memory; it means that every time we celebrate this Sacrament we participate in the mystery of the passion, death, and resurrection of Christ.

The Eucharist is the summit of God's saving action: the Lord Jesus, by becoming bread broken for us, pours upon us all of his mercy and his love, so as to renew our hearts, our lives, and our way of relating with him and with the brethren.

— General Audience, February 5, 2014

Reflection: Do you ever struggle to get something out of Mass? Pray the Stations of the Cross this week and imagine that you are actually there at Jesus' passion. Take your meditations from this time and use them to help you to experience this event at Mass.

Will We Let Ourselves?

The Church offers all the possibility of following a path of holiness, that is the path of the Christian: she brings us to encounter Jesus Christ in the sacraments, especially in confession and in the Eucharist; she communicates the Word of God to us, she lets us live in charity, in the love of God for all. Let us ask ourselves then, will we let ourselves be sanctified?

— General Audience, October 2, 2013

Reflection: The Holy Father listed several ways to experience the mercy of God, through sacraments, the Word of God, and acts of charity. Which of these ways would you like to focus on this month? Spend quality time pursuing the mercy of God.

Coming Back From a Funeral

Consequently, an evangelizer must never look like someone who has just come back from a funeral! Let us recover and deepen our enthusiasm, that "delightful and comforting joy of evangelizing, even when it is in tears that we must sow.... And may the world of our time, which is searching, sometimes with anguish, sometimes with hope, be enabled to receive the Good News not from evangelizers who are dejected, discouraged, impatient, or anxious, but from ministers of the Gospel whose lives glow with fervor, who have first received the joy of Christ."

— *Evangelii Gaudium*

Reflection: Examine your attitude lately. Are you dejected, discouraged, impatient, or anxious? Do you reflect a person who has the joy of Christ? What needs to change in your life so that you can be more joyful?

Those Merciful Hands

Our sins are in the hands of God; those merciful hands, those hands "wounded" by love. It was not by chance that Jesus willed to preserve the wounds in his hands to enable us to know and feel his mercy. And this is our strength, our hope.

— Homily, November 4, 2013

Reflection: Picture your sins in the merciful hands of God — all of your weaknesses, your deficiencies and failings. Ask God to heal you and to give you the grace and hope to help overcome them.

Where Is My Tomb?

Today I invite you to think for a moment, in silence, here: Where is my interior necrosis? Where is the dead part of my soul? Where is my tomb? Think, for a short moment.... What part of the heart can be corrupted because of my attachment to sin, one sin or another? And to remove the stone, to take away the stone of shame and allow the Lord to say to us, as he said to Lazarus: "Come out!" That all our soul might be healed, might be raised by the love of Jesus, by the power of Jesus.

He is capable of forgiving us. We all need it! All of us. We are all sinners, but we must be careful not to become corrupt! Sinners we may be, but He forgives us.

— Homily, April 6, 2014

Reflection: Consider Pope Francis' questions above. What parts of your life need healing, mercy, and resurrection? Trust in the power of Jesus to transform you.

Mary's Faith

The journey of faith thus passes through the Cross. Mary understood this from the beginning, when Herod sought to kill the newborn Jesus. But then this experience of the Cross became deeper when Jesus was rejected.

Mary was always with Jesus, she followed Jesus in the midst of the crowds, and she heard all the gossip and the nastiness of those who opposed the Lord. And she carried this cross! Mary's faith encountered misunderstanding and contempt. When Jesus' "hour" came, the hour of his passion ... Mary's faith was a little flame burning in the night, a little light flickering in the darkness.

— Address, October 12, 2013

Reflection: Imagine the scene of Jesus' passion through the eyes of Mary. What did she see? What was she thinking? How did she love those in the crowd, even in this moment? How can this help you learn to love others too?

A Providential Time

Lent comes to us as a providential time to change course, to recover the ability to react to the reality of evil which always challenges us. Lent is to be lived as a time of conversion, as a time of renewal for individuals and communities, by drawing close to God and by trustfully adhering to the Gospel.

In this way, it also allows us to look with new eyes at our brothers and sisters and their needs. That is why Lent is a favorable time to convert to the love of God and neighbor; a love that knows how to make its own the Lord's attitude of gratuitousness and mercy — who "became poor, so that by his poverty you might become rich" (cf. 2 Cor 8:9).

— General Audience, March 5, 2014

Reflection: In what ways can you look "with new eyes" at your brothers and sisters and their needs. Pray that God will allow you to look upon others with more mercy.

The Courage to Ask Jesus

[The] Gospel presents Jesus' encounter with the Samaritan woman in Sicar, near an old well where the woman went to draw water daily.... Jesus needed to encounter the Samaritan woman in order to open her heart: He asks for a drink so as to bring to light her own thirst. The woman is moved by this encounter: She asks Jesus several profound questions that we all carry within, but often ignore. We, too, have many questions to ask, but we don't have the courage to ask Jesus!

Lent, dear brothers and sisters, is the opportune time to look within ourselves, to understand our truest spiritual needs, and to ask the Lord's help in prayer.

— Angelus, March 23, 2014

Reflection: What are your needs right now? Where do you thirst for God's mercy? Turn to God in prayer and lift up your thoughts, trials, and intentions to Our Lord.

Life Is Often Wearisome

Life is often wearisome, and many times tragically so.... But what is most burdensome in life is not this: what weighs more than all of these things is a lack of love. It weighs upon us never to receive a smile, not to be welcomed. Certain silences are oppressive, even at times within families, between husbands and wives, between parents and children, among siblings. Without love, the burden becomes even heavier, intolerable.

— Address, Pilgrimage of Families, October 26, 2013

Reflection: What is one action of mercy that you can make today to help relieve the burdens of others?

The Culture of Prosperity

A globalization of indifference has developed. Almost without being aware of it, we end up being incapable of feeling compassion at the outcry of the poor, weeping for other people's pain, and feeling a need to help them, as though all this were someone else's responsibility and not our own. The culture of prosperity deadens us; we are thrilled if the market offers us something new to purchase. In the meantime, all those lives stunted for lack of opportunity seem a mere spectacle; they fail to move us.

— *Evangelii Gaudium*

Reflection: What moves you? What grabs your attention? Where do you lack compassion? Pray that God can renew your mind to care for the poor more deeply. Ask him to enliven your heart to their needs.

The Security of the Shore

The Gospel offers us the chance to live life on a higher plane, but with no less intensity: "Life grows by being given away, and it weakens in isolation and comfort. Indeed, those who enjoy life most are those who leave security on the shore and become excited by the mission of communicating life to others."

When the Church summons Christians to take up the task of evangelization, she is simply pointing to the source of authentic personal fulfilment. For "here we discover a profound law of reality: that life is attained and matures in the measure that it is offered up in order to give life to others. This is certainly what mission means."

— *Evangelii Gaudium*

Reflection: Pope Francis tells us that by sharing God's mercy with others, we will not only help others find fulfillment in Christ, we will find fulfillment as well. What area of your life can you give over more to others?

Make Him Hear the Cry of Your Heart

FEAST OF ST. GREGORY THE GREAT

It is possible for all things to be made new and different, because God remains "rich in kindness and mercy, unrelenting in forgiveness," and encourages us repeatedly to begin anew.... As St. Gregory the Great says: The wound of the soul is sin: Oh, poor wounded one, recognize your physician! Show him the wounds of your faults. Since we cannot hide from him our most secret thoughts, make him hear the cry of your heart. Move him to compassion with your tears, with your insistence beg him! Let him hear your sighs that your pain may reach him so that, at the end, he can say to you: "The Lord has forgiven your sin."

— Lenten Message, February 13, 2013,
Only Love Can Save Us

Reflection: What do we turn to in order to heal our brokenness? Another person? An addiction? Turn to God right now and show him your wounds. Make him hear the cry of your heart. He will heal you.

The Strength of the Christian

Prayer is the strength of the Christian and of every person who believes. In the weakness and frailty of our lives, we can turn to God with the confidence of children and enter into communion with him. In the face of so many wounds that hurt us and could harden our hearts, we are called to dive into the sea of prayer, which is the sea of God's boundless love, to taste his tenderness.

Lent is a time of prayer, of more intense prayer, more prolonged, more assiduous, more able to take on the needs of the brethren; intercessory prayer, to intercede before God for the many situations of poverty and suffering.

— Homily, March 5, 2014

Reflection: How is your prayer life right now? What would you like it to look like? Make a resolution to take a step forward toward a strong prayer life this month.

Placing Our Trust in God

We must be careful not to practice a formal fast, or one which, in truth, "satisfies" us because it makes us feel good about ourselves. Fasting makes sense if it questions our security, and if it also leads to some benefit for others, if it helps us to cultivate the style of the Good Samaritan, who bends down to his brother in need and takes care of him.

Fasting involves choosing a sober lifestyle, a way of life that does not waste, a way of life that does not "throw away." Fasting helps us to attune our hearts to the essential and to sharing. It is a sign of awareness and responsibility in the face of injustice, abuse, especially to the poor and the little ones, and it is a sign of the trust we place in God and in his providence.

— Homily, March 5, 2014

Reflection: Fasting allows us to feel the need for God's mercy and be more merciful to those who go hungry. What ways can you fast during this upcoming week? Find at least a small way to make a sacrifice that is out of the ordinary.

Give Freely

[Almsgiving] points to giving freely, for in almsgiving one gives something to someone from whom one does not expect to receive anything in return. Gratuitousness should be one of the characteristics of the Christian, who aware of having received everything from God gratuitously, that is, without any merit of his own, learns to give to others freely. Today gratuitousness is often not part of daily life, where everything is bought and sold. Everything is calculated and measured.

Almsgiving helps us to experience giving freely, which leads to freedom from the obsession of possessing, from the fear of losing what we have, from the sadness of one who does not wish to share his wealth with others.

— Homily, March 5, 2014

Reflection: Do you practice mercy through giving? Find an opportunity to give freely without expecting anything in return.

We Can Speak to God?

Let us hear this: it is God himself who knocks at Abraham's door and says to him: go forth, leave your land, begin to walk, and I will make of you a great people.

And this is the beginning of the Church, and within this people Jesus is born. God takes the initiative and turns his word to man, creating a bond and a new relationship with him. "But, Father, how can this be? God speaks to us?" "Yes." "And we can speak to God?" "Yes." "But can we have a conversation with God?" "Yes." This is called prayer, but it is God who started it all. Thus God forms a people with all those who listen to his Word and set themselves on the journey, trusting in him.

— General Audience, June 18, 2014

Reflection: Lectio divina (Latin for divine reading) is the practice of reading and contemplating God's Word in Scripture slowly and attentively. Through this practice we can enter into a conversation with God and come to a deeper understanding of how we can live more fully in him, applying his Word and guidance in our lives. Learn more about this practice. Be open to the conversation God wants to start with you.

It Is a Thrilling Experience

The Lord asks us to be joyous heralds of this message of mercy and hope! It is thrilling to experience the joy of spreading this good news, sharing the treasure entrusted to us, consoling broken hearts, and offering hope to our brothers and sisters experiencing darkness. It means following and imitating Jesus, who sought out the poor and sinners as a shepherd lovingly seeks his lost sheep.

— Lenten Message 2014

Reflection: How can you imitate Jesus more closely? Ask the Lord to experience his hope and mercy more intensely so that you can give this hope and mercy to others.

The Feverish Pursuit

Whenever our interior life becomes caught up in its own interests and concerns, there is no longer room for others, no place for the poor. God's voice is no longer heard, the quiet joy of his love is no longer felt, and the desire to do good fades.

This is a very real danger for believers, too. Many fall prey to it, and end up resentful, angry, and listless. That is no way to live a dignified and fulfilled life; it is not God's will for us, nor is it the life in the Spirit which has its source in the heart of the Risen Christ.

— *Evangelii Gaudium*

Reflection: Christ tells us in the Gospels, "For where your treasure is, there will your heart be also" (Lk 12:34). Where is your heart? What does it pursue? What does it get caught up in? Ask the Lord to purify your heart to seek his mercy so that you can give it to others.

Guardianship of Jesus

FEAST OF ST. JOSEPH, SPOUSE OF THE BLESSED VIRGIN MARY

Dear brothers and sisters, Joseph's mission is certainly unique and unrepeatable, because Jesus is absolutely unique. And yet, in his guardianship of Jesus, forming him to grow in age, wisdom, and grace, he is a model for every educator, especially every father....

I ask for you the grace to be ever closer to your children, allow them to grow, but be close, close! They need you, your presence, your closeness, your love. May you be for them as St. Joseph was: guardians of their growth in age, wisdom, and grace. May you guard them on their journey: be educators and walk with them. And by this closeness you will be true educators.

— General Audience, March 19, 2014

Reflection: What can you learn from St. Joseph's example of mercy toward Mary and Jesus? How can you live this out in the upcoming weeks?

No Other Way to Conquer Evil

"Behold, the Lamb of God, who takes away the sin of the world!" (Jn 1:29). The verb that is translated as "take away" literally means, "to lift up," "to take upon oneself." Jesus came into the world with a precise mission: to liberate it from the slavery of sin by taking on himself the sins of mankind. How? By loving.

There is no other way to conquer evil and sin than by the love that leads to giving up one's life for others.

— Angelus, January 19, 2014

Reflection: In Jesus' love and mercy, he took away our sins through his death on the cross. Take some time to consider what he endured for you. Consider how you can respond in love.

Called to Be Poor

We are all called to be poor, to strip us of ourselves; and to do this we must learn how to be with the poor, to share with those who lack basic necessities, to touch the flesh of Christ! The Christian is not one who speaks about the poor, no! He is one who encounters them, who looks them in the eye, who touches them.

— Address, October 4, 2013

Reflection: It's easy to help the poor from a distance. Maybe we give money to the poor or our gently used clothing. This is good, but ask God for the courage to encounter them face-to-face. Ask him for the ability to give his mercy and to see them as he does. These encounters will give you the joy that comes with sharing your life with others.

Many Try to Escape

Many try to escape from others and take refuge in the comfort of their privacy or in a small circle of close friends, renouncing the realism of the social aspect of the Gospel. For just as some people want a purely spiritual Christ, without flesh and without the cross, they also want their interpersonal relationships provided by sophisticated equipment, by screens and systems which can be turned on and off on command.

— *Evangelii Gaudium*

Reflection: Do you ever try to escape from others? Do you find yourself choosing media and electronics over true and real relationships? Find ways to break out of these habits so that you can give and receive mercy in relationships with others.

How Important This Is!

But the most important thing is to walk together by working together, by helping one another, by asking forgiveness, by acknowledging one's mistakes and asking for forgiveness, and also by accepting the apologies of others by forgiving — how important this is!

— Address, October 4, 2013

Reflection: Who do you need to forgive? Who do you need to ask for forgiveness? Experience the joy of giving and receiving mercy.

Servant of Mercy

God forgives every man in his sovereign mercy, but he himself willed that those who belong to Christ and to the Church receive forgiveness by means of the ministers of the community. Through the apostolic ministry the mercy of God reaches me, my faults are forgiven and joy is bestowed on me....

The Church, who is holy and at the same time in need of penitence, accompanies us on the journey of conversion throughout our life. The Church is not mistress of the power of the keys, but a servant of the ministry of mercy and rejoices every time she can offer this divine gift.

— General Audience, November 20, 2013

Reflection: Jesus established the Sacrament of Reconciliation through the Church so that the Church could accompany us in our journey of conversion. Take time this week to experience God's mercy in this great sacrament.

With the Humility and Courage of Mary

Feast of the Annunciation of the Lord

Do we think that Jesus' incarnation is simply a past event which has nothing to do with us personally? Believing in Jesus means giving him our flesh with the humility and courage of Mary, so that he can continue to dwell in our midst.

It means giving him our hands, to caress the little ones and the poor; our feet, to go forth and meet our brothers and sisters; our arms, to hold up the weak and to work in the Lord's vineyard; our minds, to think and act in the light of the Gospel; and especially to offer our hearts to love and to make choices in accordance with God's will.

— Address, Marian Day, October 12, 2013

Reflection: At the Annunciation, Mary's courageous "yes" brought Jesus to earth in the flesh. What "yes" do you need to make this week to bring Jesus' love and mercy to earth?

This Makes Us Grow

He always forgives us. And it is precisely this that makes us grow as God's people, as the Church: not our cleverness, not our merits — we are a small thing, it's not that — but the daily experience of how much the Lord wishes us well and takes care of us. It is this that makes us feel that we are truly his, in his hands, and makes us grow in communion with him and with one another.

To be Church is to feel oneself in the hands of God, who is father and loves us, caresses us, waits for us and makes us feel his tenderness. And this is very beautiful!

— General Audience, June 18, 2014

Reflection: As Christians, growth doesn't always come from doing everything right, but through failing and trying again. We can concentrate so intently on success that we overlook the value of failing and turning to the Lord for his help and mercy. Put yourself and all of your weaknesses in the hands of the Father.

Listen to Jesus

Listen to Jesus! "But, Father, I do listen to Jesus, I listen a lot!" "Yes? What do you listen to?" "I listen to the radio, I listen to the television, I listen to people gossip." We listen to so many things throughout the day, so many things....

But I ask you a question: Do we take a little time each day to listen to Jesus, to listen to Jesus' word? Do we have the Gospels at home? And do we listen to Jesus each day in the Gospel? So we read a passage from the Gospel?... I suggest that each day you take a few minutes and read a nice passage of the Gospel and hear what happens there.

— Homily, March 16, 2014

Reflection: To give God's mercy, we must open our hearts to receive it from God first. Perhaps this Lent you can find one thing in your life to stop listening to and take up Pope Francis' challenge to read the Gospels each day. Make Jesus the most important influence in your life.

Evangelized by the Poor

We need to let ourselves be evangelized by [the poor]. The New Evangelization is an invitation to acknowledge the saving power at work in their lives and to put them at the center of the Church's pilgrim way. We are called to find Christ in them, to lend our voice to their causes, but also to be their friends, to listen to them, to speak for them, and to embrace the mysterious wisdom which God wishes to share with us through them.

— *Evangelii Gaudium*

Reflection: Do you have friendships with the poor? What does having a friendship with the poor look like practically? What opportunities are available to you in your Church and community?

Am I Like One of Them?

[In the reading of the Passion], we [hear] many, many names. The group of leaders, some priests, the Pharisees, the teachers of the law, who had decided to kill Jesus. They were waiting for the chance to arrest him. Am I like one of them?

— Homily, April 13, 2014

Reflection: Read Mark 14:1—15:47. Imagine that you are there at Jesus' death and resurrection. What is God saying to you about mercy as you picture the scene? Who are you before the Lord?

No Christianity Without the Cross

Christianity is not a philosophical doctrine, it is not a program of life that enables one to be well formed and to make peace. These are its consequences. Christianity is a person, a person lifted up on the cross. A person who emptied himself to save us. He took on sin. And so just as in the desert sin was lifted up, here God made man was lifted up for us. And all of our sins were there.... [Therefore] one cannot understand Christianity without understanding this profound humiliation of the Son of God, who humbled himself and made himself a servant unto death on the cross....

Thanks to the mercy of God, we glory in Christ Crucified. And that is why there is no Christianity without the Cross, and there is no Cross without Jesus Christ.

— Homily, *Domus Sanctae Marthae*, April 8, 2014

Reflection: Do you ever get caught up in being a nice person or studying the teachings of the faith while losing track of your relationship with Jesus? Pray the Stations of the Cross this week to center yourself on the mercy of God.

He Became Poor

[God] does not reveal himself cloaked in worldly power and wealth but rather in weakness and poverty: "though He was rich, yet for your sake he became poor...." Christ, the eternal Son of God, one with the Father in power and glory, chose to be poor; he came amongst us and drew near to each of us; he set aside his glory and emptied himself so that he could be like us in all things (cf. Phil 2:7; Heb 4:15).

God's becoming man is a great mystery! But the reason for all this is his love, a love which is grace, generosity, a desire to draw near, a love which does not hesitate to offer itself in sacrifice for the beloved.

— Lenten Message 2014

Reflection: Take some time to reflect on God's willingness to lower himself to become man. In light of Christ's own example, where is God calling you to be poor in your life? Where is he calling you to sacrifice for others?

At That Critical Moment

On the cross, when Jesus endured in his own flesh the dramatic encounter of the sin of the world and God's mercy, he could feel at his feet the consoling presence of his mother and his friend. At that crucial moment, before fully accomplishing the work which his Father had entrusted to him, Jesus said to Mary: "Woman, here is your son." Then he said to his beloved friend: "Here is your mother" (Jn 19:26-27).

These words of the dying Jesus are not chiefly the expression of his devotion and concern for his mother; rather, they are a revelatory formula which manifests the mystery of a special saving mission. Jesus left us his mother to be our mother.

— *Evangelii Gaudium*

Reflection: During his greatest moment of mercy, Jesus gave us his mother to be our mother. What is your relationship with Mary like? Do you consider her to be your mother? Take some time to invite her to be a more intimate part of your life.

Imagine That You Are There

We might well ask ourselves just one question: Who am I? Who am I, before my Lord? Who am I, before Jesus who enters Jerusalem amid the enthusiasm of the crowd? Am I ready to express my joy, to praise him? Or do I stand back? Who am I, before the suffering Jesus?

— Homily, April 13, 2014

Reflection: In order to accept the mercy of God, we must have the courage to accept him publically. Consider the scene of Palm Sunday. Place yourself in the scene and imagine that you are there. Where do you find yourself? Who are you, before the Lord?

The Good Thief

The thief who went astray in his life, but now repents, clings to the crucified Jesus and begs him: "Remember me, when you come into your kingdom" (Lk 23:42). Jesus promises him: "Today you will be with me in paradise" (v. 43), in his kingdom. Jesus speaks only a word of forgiveness, not of condemnation; whenever anyone finds the courage to ask for this forgiveness, the Lord does not let such a petition go unheard.

— Homily, November 24, 2013

Reflection: Read the account of the good thief in Luke 23:29-43 and put yourself in the story as the thief. In our relationship with God, it is important to recognize that we are sinners before the Lord, but sinners who are loved and forgiven, not condemned. What does Jesus say to you as you picture the scene?

Mary Kept Watch

Through the night of Holy Saturday, Mary kept watch. Her flame, small but bright, remained burning until the dawn of the Resurrection. And when she received word that the tomb was empty, her heart was filled with the joy of faith: Christian faith in the death and resurrection of Jesus Christ.

Faith always brings us to joy, and Mary is the mother of joy! May she teach us to take the path of joy, to experience this joy! That was the high point — this joy, this meeting of Jesus and Mary, and we can imagine what it was like. Their meeting was the high point of Mary's journey of faith, and that of the whole Church.

What is our faith like? Like Mary, do we keep it burning even at times of difficulty, in moments of darkness? Do I feel the joy of faith?

— Address, Marian Day, October 12, 2013

Reflection: Consider the Holy Father's questions, above. Ask Mary for her intercession to help you imitate her love of Jesus.

Boundless Mercy

God is infinite love, boundless mercy, and that Love has conquered evil at its root through the death and resurrection of Christ. This is the Gospel, the Good News: God's love has won! Christ died on the cross for our sins and rose again. With him we can fight evil and conquer every day.

Do we believe this or not?... But that "yes" has to become part of life! If I believe that Jesus has conquered evil and saved me, I must follow along the path of Jesus for my whole life.

— Address, Meeting with Young People,
October 4, 2013

Reflection: God's mercy is boundless. Whatever you are facing, God's love is there to conquer it. Think about your own personal trials and battles. Say yes to the love of God in each situation.

A Vital Power

Christ's resurrection is not an event of the past; it contains a vital power which has permeated this world. Where all seems to be dead, signs of the Resurrection suddenly spring up. It is an irresistible force.

Often it seems that God does not exist: all around us we see persistent injustice, evil, indifference, and cruelty. But it is also true that in the midst of darkness something new always springs to life and sooner or later produces fruit.

— *Evangelii Gaudium*

Reflection: When we trust in him, God's mercy and grace are working through us even though we can't see it. He is bringing about change in our hearts, minds, and souls. Place your trust most deeply in him, especially when you can't see or feel him working.

Wellspring of Mercy

I cannot say: I forgive my sins. Forgiveness is asked for, is asked of another, and in confession we ask for forgiveness from Jesus. Forgiveness is not the fruit of our own efforts but rather a gift, it is a gift of the Holy Spirit who fills us with the wellspring of mercy and of grace that flows unceasingly from the open heart of the Crucified and Risen Christ.

— General Audience, February 19, 2014

Reflection: The mercy of God is a gift. We must approach it with humility, not a sense of entitlement. Ask God for the humility to receive mercy in his way, not our own. What is he is calling you to do as a result of his forgiveness?

Pray for Me

Jesus prays for us! Jesus who prays, Jesus the man-God who prays! And he prays for us: he prays for me, he prays for you, and for each one of us....

When — [whether] at church, at home with our families — we are in need or have problems, we say "pray for me," we have to say the same to Jesus: "Lord, pray for me."... We must have this faith that Jesus, in this moment, intercedes before the Father for us, for each one of us. And when we pray, we are asking: "Jesus, help me, Jesus, give me strength, solve this problem, forgive me!"

— Homily, *Domus Sanctae Marthae*, June 3, 2014

Reflection: Where do you turn to when you have problems? Do you first try to solve them yourself? Do you turn to others to solve them for you? Turn to God first. Let him be the first to hear your needs.

God Asks Everything of Us

In every activity of evangelization, the primacy always belongs to God, who has called us to cooperate with him and who leads us on by the power of his Spirit. The real newness is the newness which God himself mysteriously brings about and inspires, provokes, guides, and accompanies in a thousand ways.... God asks everything of us, yet at the same time he offers everything to us.

— *Evangelii Gaudium*

Reflection: How is God accompanying you right now? Where is he leading you? God asks so much of us, but he's also given us the gift of mercy through his Son and the gift of the Holy Spirit to guide us. Trust in them.

This Is Unacceptable!

Today, unfortunately, the speculative economy makes the poor ever poorer, depriving them of the essentials, such as housing and employment. This is unacceptable! Those who live solidarity don't accept it, and they take action.

And this word, "solidarity," many people want to eliminate it from the dictionary, because some cultures see it as a bad word. No! Solidarity is a Christian word! And this is why you are the family of the homeless, friends of disabled persons, who — when loved — express great humanity.

— Address to the Sant'Egidio Community,
June 15, 2014

Reflection: How can you be in solidarity with the poor? Are you willing to open your eyes and really see the poverty in your area? Are you willing to consider how you can serve?

He Is a New Man

The apostle Thomas personally experiences this mercy of God, which has a concrete face, the face of Jesus, the risen Jesus. Thomas does not believe it when the other apostles tell him: "We have seen the Lord." It isn't enough for him that Jesus had foretold it, promised it: "On the third day I will rise." He wants to see, he wants to put his hand in the place of the nails and in Jesus' side....

[Thomas] lets himself be enveloped by divine mercy; he sees it before his eyes, in the wounds of Christ's hands and feet and in his open side, and he discovers trust: he is a new man, no longer an unbeliever, but a believer.

— Homily, Divine Mercy Sunday, April 7, 2013

Reflection: Like Thomas, we need to experience God's love and mercy for ourselves. How have you discovered God's mercy in the past? Through a retreat? The Stations of the Cross? The support of a friend? Take some time to recollect how you've experienced the Lord's mercy, and ask him to remind you of how much he loves you.

The Price of Our Salvation

We must remember that the principal agent in the forgiveness of sins is the Holy Spirit. In his first appearance to the apostles, in the Upper Room, the risen Jesus made the gesture of breathing on them, saying: "Receive the Holy Spirit. If you forgive the sins of any, they are forgiven; if you retain the sins of any, they are retained" (Jn 20:22,23)....
But before making this gesture of breathing and transmitting the Holy Spirit, Jesus reveals the wounds in his hands and side: these wounds represent the price of our salvation.

— General Audience, November 20, 2013

Reflection: Jesus asks us to repent from our sins, but within the context of his merciful wounds that he suffered for our sake. Meditate on his cross. Ask the Holy Spirit for guidance as you consider your sins.

The Stench of a Person

We are all sinners! But if we become very attached to these tombs and guard them within us, and do not will that our whole heart rise again to life, we become corrupted and our soul begins to give off, as Martha says, an "odor" (Jn 11:39), the stench of a person who is attached to sin.
— Homily, April 6, 2014

Reflection: Where does your life stink? What needs to be resurrected? Where are you attached to sin? Don't separate these areas from the mercy of God. Open them up to the power of the Lord.

Do We Welcome Sinners?

The Lord wants us to belong to a Church that knows how to open her arms and welcome everyone, that is not a house for the few, but a house for everyone, where all can be renewed, transformed, sanctified by his love, the strongest and the weakest, sinners, the indifferent, those who feel discouraged or lost....

Are we a Church that calls and welcomes sinners with open arms, that gives courage and hope, or are we a Church closed in on herself? Are we a Church where the love of God dwells, where one cares for the other, where one prays for the others?

— General Audience, October 2, 2013

Reflection: Consider the questions Pope Francis asks of us. Make a practical resolution to answer the call to be a more welcoming and merciful Church.

Participation in the Love of the Father

Our sonship is fidelity, gratitude, and participation. And fidelity to the love of God who loved us first, created us and gave up his only-begotten Son, Jesus Christ, for our sake.

It is gratitude for his fatherly mercy, the joy that opens eyes and hearts to the presence, the goodness and the beauty of our brothers and sisters.

It is the participation in the love of the Father, of the Son, and of the Holy Spirit, who brings us to share one another's joy and sorrow, happiness and the suffering, prosperity and adversity.

— General Audience, June 4, 2014

Reflection: By sharing in God's mercy, joy, and happiness, as well as his sorrow and adversity, we learn to share in the joy and sorrow of others. St. Paul tells us to "Rejoice with those who rejoice, weep with those who weep" (Rom 12:15). Who could you rejoice with right now? Who do you need to mourn with?

The Poor Teach Us

FEAST OF ST. BENEDICT JOSEPH LABRÉ

The poor are not just people to whom we can give something. They have much to offer us and to teach us. How much we have to learn from the wisdom of the poor! Think about it: Several hundred years ago, a saint, Benedict Joseph Labré, who lived on the streets of Rome from the alms he received, became a spiritual guide to all sorts of people, including nobles and prelates.

In a very real way, the poor are our teachers. They show us that people's value is not measured by their possessions or how much money they have in the bank. A poor person, a person lacking material possessions, always maintains his or her dignity. The poor can teach us much about humility and trust in God.

— World Youth Day 2014

Reflection: Have you heard of St. Benedict Joseph Labré? Read a brief biography of his life. What can you learn from his poverty? Where are you called to learn from the poor?

Life Sometimes Wounds Us

The road to Emmaus thus becomes a symbol of our journey of faith: the Scriptures and the Eucharist are the indispensable elements for encountering the Lord. We too often go to Sunday Mass with our worries, difficulties, and disappointments.... Life sometimes wounds us, and we go away feeling sad, toward our "Emmaus," turning our backs on God's plan. We distance ourselves from God. But the Liturgy of the Word welcomes us.

— *Regina Caeli*, May 4, 2014

Reflection: If Jesus were walking alongside you, what would he say to you? In what area of your life would he offer encouragement? What area would he ask you to change? Ask God for the courage to encounter his mercy in the face of these challenges.

To Draw Near

From the Gospel narratives we are able to understand the closeness, the goodness, the tenderness with which Jesus drew in the suffering people and consoled them, comforted them, and often healed them. By our Teacher's example, we too are called to draw near, to share the conditions of the people we meet.

— Address, June 14, 2014

Reflection: How can you draw near to share in the condition of those you meet? How can you listen more attentively? How can you comfort them? How can you follow-up with them?

Not a Path of Revenge

The Lord always goes ahead, making the way of a Christian known to us. It is not ... a path of revenge. The Christian spirit is something else, the Lord says. It is the spirit that he showed us in the most important moment of his life, in his passion: a spirit of humility, a spirit of meekness.

— Homily, *Domus Sanctae Marthae*, October 1, 2013

Reflection: How does the Christian spirit change your life? Where does your life look different than others? Can others tell that God's mercy is an integral part of your life?

By the Power of These Wounds

The Holy Spirit brings us God's pardon "by passing through" Jesus' wounds. These wounds he wished to keep; even now in heaven he is showing the Father the wounds by which he redeemed us. By the power of these wounds, our sins are pardoned: thus Jesus gave his life for our peace, for our joy, for the gift of grace in our souls, for the forgiveness of our sins. It is very, very beautiful to look at Jesus in this way!

— General Audience, November 20, 2013

Reflection: Jesus retained the wounds of the cross because they are great signs of his love for us. Think about the suffering Jesus endured on the cross and the wounds he bore for our sake. Take time to contemplate that Jesus suffered in this way to give you mercy.

Anoint Us to Become His Children

Through the anointing of the Spirit, our human nature is sealed with the holiness of Jesus Christ, and we are enabled to love our brothers and sisters with the same love which God has for us. We ought, therefore, to show concrete signs of humility, fraternity, forgiveness, and reconciliation. These signs are the prerequisite of a true, stable, and lasting peace. Let us ask the Father to anoint us so that we may fully become his children, ever more conformed to Christ, and may learn to see one another as brothers and sisters.

— Homily, May 24, 2014

Reflection: Are we only concerned about those we know, our relatives, our friends, our fellow faithful Catholics? Does God's mercy change the way we look at others? Are we open to everyone? Ask God the Father to anoint you with his mercy, to change your heart and mind.

Looking Death in the Face

Think well on this: The one who practices mercy does not fear death! Do you agree? Shall we say it together so as not to forget it? The one who practices mercy does not fear death. And why does he not fear it? Because he looks death in the face in the wounds of his brothers and sisters, and he overcomes it with the love of Jesus Christ.

— General Audience, November 27, 2013

Reflection: Have you ever visited someone who is courageously fighting cancer? They give us so much strength! They help us put things into perspective. Visit someone who is ill. They will help you overcome your fears.

Becoming Fully Human

We become fully human when we become more than human, when we let God bring us beyond ourselves in order to attain the fullest truth of our being. Here we find the source and inspiration of all our efforts at evangelization. For if we have received the love which restores meaning to our lives, how can we fail to share that love with others?

— *Evangelii Gaudium*

Reflection: How does God's mercy make us more human? How does a real encounter with his mercy cause us to share this mercy with others? Where is God calling you to share his mercy next?

Wellspring of Our Hope

If we think that things are not going to change, we need to recall that Jesus Christ has triumphed over sin and death, and is now almighty. Jesus Christ truly lives....

The Gospel tells us that when the first disciples went forth to preach, "the Lord worked with them and confirmed the message" (Mk 16:20). The same thing happens today. We are invited to discover this, to experience it. Christ, risen and glorified, is the wellspring of our hope, and he will not deprive us of the help we need to carry out the mission which he has entrusted to us.

— *Evangelii Gaudium*

Reflection: What help do you need today? Turn to God and let him know your needs and fears. Take hope that he will help you to be an instrument of his mercy.

When One Is in Line to Go to Confession

Do not be afraid of confession! When one is in line to go to confession, one feels all these things, even shame, but then when one finishes confession one leaves free, grand, beautiful, forgiven, candid, happy. This is the beauty of confession!

— General Audience, February 19, 2014

Reflection: There is freedom in the Lord's mercy. Don't be afraid. Go to confession this week.

Jesus' Relationship
With His Disciples

The Evangelist John presents us ... with the image of Jesus the Good Shepherd. In contemplating this page of the Gospel, we can understand the kind of relationship that Jesus had with his disciples: a relationship based on tenderness, love, mutual knowledge, and the promise of an immeasurable gift: "I came," Jesus said, "that they may have life, and have it abundantly" (Jn 10:10)....

I invite everyone to place their trust in the Lord who guides us. But he not only guides us: he accompanies us, he walks with us. Let us listen to his Word with minds and hearts opened, to nourish our faith, enlighten our conscience, and follow the teaching of the Gospel.

— *Regina Caeli*, May 11, 2014

Reflection: What area of your life is not abundant? Jesus promises that committing our lives to his mercy and following his teachings will lead to fulfillment. Pray that God will continue to walk with you in your weaknesses and failings.

The Dawn of Easter Breaks Forth

Every time we ask forgiveness of one another for our sins against other Christians, and every time we find the courage to grant and receive such forgiveness, we experience the Resurrection!

Every time we put behind us our long-standing prejudices and find the courage to build new fraternal relationships, we confess that Christ is truly risen!

Every time we reflect on the future of the Church in the light of her vocation to unity, the dawn of Easter breaks forth!

— Address, Pilgrimage to the Holy Land,
May 25, 2014

Reflection: Where do you experience the Resurrection in your life? Where do you need to experience it more? Seek his mercy by asking for forgiveness.

Jesus, I Trust in You

Many times we trust a doctor: it is good, because the doctor is there to cure us; we trust in a person: brothers and sisters can help us. It is good to have this human trust among ourselves.

But we forget about trust in the Lord: this is the key to success in life. Trust in the Lord, let us trust in the Lord! "Lord, look at my life: I'm in the dark, I have this struggle, I have this sin . . ."; everything we have: "Look at this: I trust in you!" And this is a risk we must take: to trust in him, and he never disappoints.

— Homily, January 19, 2014

Reflection: When Jesus appeared to St. Faustina, he gave her a simple phrase to respond to Jesus' mercy. The phrase is: "Jesus, I trust in you." Think of all your current struggles and challenges, then, repeat: "Jesus, I trust in you! Jesus, I trust in you! Jesus, I trust in you!"

To Enter His Wounds

How can I find the wounds of Jesus today? I cannot see them as Thomas saw them [who disbelieved until he put his fingers in the wounds of the Risen Christ]. I find them in doing works of mercy, in giving to the body — to the body and to the soul, but I stress the body — of your injured brethren, for they are hungry, thirsty, naked, humiliated, slaves, in prison, in hospital. These are the wounds of Jesus in our day.

We must touch the wounds of Jesus, caress them. We must heal the wounds of Jesus with tenderness.... What Jesus asks us to do with our works of mercy is what Thomas asked: to enter his wounds.

— Homily, *Domus Sanctae Marthae*,
July 3, 2013

Reflection: To encounter the poor is to encounter Christ. To give mercy is to partake of the experience of God's mercy. Don't underestimate your need to give to others. It is in giving mercy that we learn to receive it as well.

Our Deepest Needs

Sometimes we lose our enthusiasm for mission because we forget that the Gospel responds to our deepest needs, since we were created for what the Gospel offers us: friendship with Jesus and love of our brothers and sisters. If we succeed in expressing adequately and with beauty the essential content of the Gospel, surely this message will speak to the deepest yearnings of people's hearts.

— *Evangelii Gaudium*

Reflection: Do we let the Gospel answer our deepest needs, our need to be loved, to be fulfilled, to have meaning and purpose? Or do we try to meet these needs with other things?

The Sweetness of Our Lady

We are in need today of the sweetness of Our Lady to understand the things that Jesus asks of us. It is not an easy list to put into practice: love your enemies, do good, give without hoping for anything in return, to him who strikes you offer the other cheek, to him who takes your cloak offer your tunic as well. These are heavy demands. But all of them were lived by Our Lady in her own way.

— Homily, *Domus Sanctae Marthae*, Feast of the
Holy Name of Mary, September 12, 2013

Reflection: Mary lived in poverty under the oppressive government of the Roman Empire. She constantly had opportunities to put love into practice, both in the grind of her daily life as a woman of poverty and when enduring the demands of the government. Ask Mary to teach you the way of Jesus. Ask her to help you learn to think and act with mercy.

Spiritual Worldliness Camouflaged

Any Church community, if it thinks it can comfortably go its own way without creative concern and effective cooperation in helping the poor to live with dignity and reaching out to everyone, will also risk breaking down, however much it may talk about social issues or criticize governments. It will easily drift into a spiritual worldliness camouflaged by religious practices, unproductive meetings and empty talk.

— *Evangelii Gaudium*

Reflection: Is your parish comfortable? Does it risk breaking down? What's one step you can make to creatively and effectively help the poor within your own parish boundaries?

Mary's Magnificat

The model of this spiritual disposition [of moving forward in hope], of this way of being and journeying in life, is the Virgin Mary. A simple girl from the country who carries within her heart the fullness of hope in God! In her womb, God's hope took flesh, it became man, it became history: Jesus Christ.

Her Magnificat is the canticle of the People of God on a journey, and of all men and women who hope in God and in the power of his mercy. Let us allow ourselves to be guided by her, she who is mother, a mamma, and knows how to guide us.

— Angelus, December 1, 2013

Reflection: Read Mary's Magnificat in Luke 1:46-55. Contemplate the way that she receives God's mercy. How can you follow her example?

The Last Judgment

He identified himself with [the most needy], in the well-known parable of the Last Judgment, in which he says, "For I was hungry and you gave me food, I was thirsty and you gave me drink, I was a stranger and you welcomed me, I was naked and you clothed me, I was sick and you visited me, I was in prison and you came to me ... 'as you did it to one of the least of these my brethren, you did it to me'" (Mt 25:35-36,40).

— General Audience, November 27, 2013

Reflection: Picture yourself before God's judgment at the end of your life. How did you measure up to Jesus' command recounted above? Having received his grace and mercy in this life, did you extend it to others? How do you want your life to change now so that you are serving Jesus in the least of his brethren?

Agents of Mercy

God's mercy can make even the driest land become a garden, can restore life to dry bones (cf. Ez 37:1-14).... Let us be renewed by God's mercy, let us be loved by Jesus, let us enable the power of his love to transform our lives too; and let us become agents of this mercy, channels through which God can water the earth, protect all creation, and make justice and peace flourish.

— *Urbi et Orbi*, Easter, March 31, 2013

Reflection: What are some of the "dry bones" in your life? Think of a situation that you have been praying for but that seems as dry and unfruitful as ever. Recommit yourself to praying for God's mercy in this situation, and ask him to use you as a channel of that mercy.

What Is the Measure of God?

The charity of Christ, welcomed with an open heart, changes us, transforms us, renders us capable of loving not according to human measure, always limited, but according to the measure of God. And what is the measure of God? Without measure! The measure of God is without measure....

And so we become capable of loving even those who do not love us: and this is not easy. To love someone who doesn't love us.... It's not easy! Because if we know that a person doesn't like us, then we also tend to bear ill will. But no! We must love even someone who doesn't love us!

Opposing evil with good, with pardon, with sharing, with welcome. Thanks to Jesus and to his Spirit, even our life becomes "bread broken" for our brothers. And living like this we discover true joy!

— Angelus, June 22, 2014

Reflection: Do you know someone who doesn't like you? Have you ever tried to love them? What difficulties arose? God's mercy and unconditional love can help us overcome these obstacles. Don't stop trying to love those who don't like you.

By Fits and Starts

And I ask myself: Am I a Christian by fits and starts, or am I a Christian full-time? Our culture of the ephemeral, the relative, also takes its toll on the way we live our faith. God asks us to be faithful to him, daily, in our everyday life.

— Homily, October 13, 2013

Reflection: Our culture tells us that we don't have to be faithful if we don't feel like it. Do you take time to be faithful to God in prayer each day? Are you faithful to the teachings of the Church, even when the situation is difficult? Where do you need to grow in greater fidelity to God?

Proclamation of Joy

Jesus teaches us that the Good News, which he brings, is not reserved to one part of humanity, it is to be communicated to everyone. It is a proclamation of joy destined for those who are waiting for it, but also for all those who perhaps are no longer waiting for anything and haven't even the strength to seek and to ask.

— Angelus, January 26, 2014

Reflection: So often we view evangelization as something that we impose on others. Something that is forced and overbearing. But, ultimately, evangelization is an act of mercy if we do it with love and the perspective of truly helping others. What's your perspective on evangelization? Ask God for his.

Faith to Move Mountains

We all know people who are simple, humble, but whose faith is so strong it can move mountains! Let us think, for example, of some mothers and fathers who face very difficult situations; or of some sick, and even gravely ill, people who transmit serenity to those who come to visit them. These people, because of their faith, do not boast about what they do, rather, as Jesus asks in the Gospel, they say, "We are unworthy servants; we have only done what was our duty" (Lk 17:10). How many people among us have such strong, humble faith, and what good they do!

— Angelus, October 6, 2013

Reflection: Which people in your life have a strong and humble faith? How does their faith, even in their weakness, encourage you?

A Place of Mercy

Being Church means being God's people, in accordance with the great plan of his fatherly love. This means that we are to be God's leaven in the midst of humanity. It means proclaiming and bringing God's salvation into our world, which often goes astray and needs to be encouraged, given hope and strengthened on the way.

The Church must be a place of mercy freely given, where everyone can feel welcomed, loved, forgiven, and encouraged to live the good life of the Gospel.

— *Evangelii Gaudium*

Reflection: What does it mean for your parish to be a place of mercy? Have you ever thought of greeting people at the door? What about being a part of the committee to welcome new parishioners? What about saying one encouraging comment to someone each week after Mass?

Patience Is a Virtue of God

True joy comes from a profound harmony between persons, something which we all feel in our hearts and which makes us experience the beauty of togetherness, of mutual support along life's journey. But the basis of this feeling of deep joy is the presence of God, the presence of God in the family and his love, which is welcoming, merciful, and respectful toward all. And above all, a love which is patient: patience is a virtue of God, and he teaches us how to cultivate it in family life, how to be patient, and lovingly so, with each other.

— Homily, October 27, 2013

Reflection: Bearing wrongs patiently is a spiritual work of mercy. What is God asking you to bear at work, in your family, in your neighborhood, at your parish?

Goodness Always Re-emerges

However dark things are, goodness always re-emerges and spreads. Each day in our world beauty is born anew; it rises transformed through the storms of history. Values always tend to reappear under new guises, and human beings have arisen time after time from situations that seemed doomed. Such is the power of the Resurrection, and all who evangelize are instruments of that power.

— *Evangelii Gaudium*

Reflection: What is your favorite story about God acting powerfully in our world? Is it something that happened to you personally or to a friend? Is it a story from Scripture or a saint? Remind yourself that God can do amazing things! Trust in the power of his mercy as you spread the faith to others.

When You Are Sad

Dear brothers and sisters, the Word of God and the Eucharist fill us with joy, always. Remember it well! When you are sad, take up the Word of God. When you are down, take up the Word of God and go to Sunday Mass and receive Communion, to participate in the mystery of Jesus. The Word of God, the Eucharist: they fill us with joy.

— *Regina Caeli*, May 4, 2014

Reflection: When you are sad, what do you turn to? Does it give you long-term happiness or just momentary pleasure? Turn to God's mercy. It will not fail you.

A Malicious Excuse

Some people do not commit themselves to mission because they think that nothing will change and that it is useless to make the effort. They think: "Why should I deny myself my comforts and pleasures if I won't see any significant result?" This attitude makes it impossible to be a missionary. It is only a malicious excuse for remaining caught up in comfort, laziness, vague dissatisfaction, and empty selfishness.

— *Evangelii Gaudium*

Reflection: Do you lack faith that God can change a situation? Examine your life right now. What prevents you from being a strong witness for him? What excuses are you making? Trust in the power of God's mercy to change you and the people around you.

Path of Poverty

For everyone, even for our society that is showing signs of fatigue, if we want to save ourselves from sinking, it is necessary to follow the path of poverty. That does not mean misery — this idea should be refuted — it means knowing how to share, how to be more in solidarity with those in need, to entrust oneself more to God and less to our human efforts.

— Address at Assisi, October 4, 2013

Reflection: How can you follow the path of poverty? Do you need a poverty of spirit where you rely less on your own efforts? Do you need a poverty of material goods where you learn to live with less?

No One Can Remain Indifferent

All who accept the life of Christ and live in him acknowledge God as Father and give themselves completely to him, loving him above all things. The reconciled person sees in God the Father of all, and, as a consequence, is spurred on to live a life of fraternity open to all.... This is the reason why no one can remain indifferent before the lot of our brothers and sisters.

— World Day of Peace Message, January 1, 2014

Reflection: Do you view others as brothers and sisters, or do you remain indifferent before their needs? When we accept God's mercy fully into our lives, everything changes, including our relationship to others. Pray for a deeper commitment to him and a deeper relationship with those around you.

The Power of Confirmation

[Confirmation] unites us more firmly to Christ, it renders our bond with the Church more perfect, and it gives us a special strength of the Holy Spirit to spread and defend the faith.... For this reason, it is important to take care that our children, our young people, receive this sacrament. We all take care that they are baptized, and this is good, but perhaps we do not take so much care to ensure that they are confirmed....

Let us think a little, each one of us: Do we truly care whether our children, our young people, receive confirmation? This is important, it is important! And if you have children or adolescents at home who have not yet received it and are at the age to do so, do everything possible to ensure that they complete their Christian initiation and receive the power of the Holy Spirit.

— General Audience, January 29, 2014

Reflection: Confirmation is so important as a means of grace that helps equip us to instruct the ignorant, which is a spiritual work of mercy. How is your parish's confirmation program? Is there anything you can do to help prepare young people for this sacrament so that they are also empowered to go out and instruct the ignorant? Can you take a moment to pray for them right now?

We Are Completely in God's Hands

Jesus predicts that his disciples will have to suffer painful trials and persecution for his sake. He reassures them, however, saying: "Not a hair of your head will perish" (Lk 21:18). This reminds us that we are completely in God's hands! The trials we encounter for our faith and our commitment to the Gospel are occasions to give witness; we must not distance ourselves from the Lord, but instead abandon ourselves even more to him, to the power of his Spirit and his grace.

— Angelus, November 17, 2013

Reflection: What trials and persecutions are you facing right now? Ask the Lord to draw near to you in your suffering. Ask him to help you remember his suffering and his mercy in these times.

Two Years, Twenty Years, Forty Years?

I would like to ask you — but don't say it aloud, everyone respond in his heart: When was the last time you made your confession? Everyone think about it ... two days, two weeks, two years, twenty years, forty years? Everyone count, everyone say, "When was the last time I went to confession?" And if much time has passed, do not lose another day. Go, the priest will be good. Jesus is there, and Jesus is more benevolent than priests. Jesus receives you; he receives you with so much love. Be courageous and go to confession!

— General Audience, February 19, 2014

Reflection: When is the last time that you went to confession? Count the weeks ... or years. Don't be afraid to encounter the mercy of the Lord through this great sacrament.

Mary's Gaze!

Mary's gaze! How important this is! How many things can we say with a look! Affection, encouragement, compassion, love, but also disapproval, envy, pride, and even hatred. Often a look says more than words; it says what words do not or dare not say.

At whom is the Virgin Mary looking? She is looking at each and every one of us. And how does she look at us? She looks at us as a Mother, with tenderness, mercy, and love.

— Message, October 12, 2013

Reflection: What does your look say about you? Do you look upon others with mercy, or does your glance convey a sense of disapproval, or superiority, or boredom? Take up Mary's example and look on others with love.

Deeply Moved

We incarnate the duty of hearing the cry of the poor when we are deeply moved by the suffering of others. Let us listen to what God's word teaches us about mercy, and allow that word to resound in the life of the Church. The Gospel tells us, "Blessed are the merciful, because they shall obtain mercy" (Mt 5:7).

— *Evangelii Gaudium*

Reflection: It's in giving that we receive. When we make acts of mercy, we in turn receive mercy, both from the person we help and from God. Allow yourself to really hear the cry of the needy, whether within your own home, neighborhood, or the larger world.

To Give Space Is to Pray

[When we put aside our own thinking,] the Spirit grows and develops within us, and we experience how true the words of Jesus are that are reported in the Gospel of Matthew, "Do not be anxious how you are to speak or what you are to say; for what you are to say will be given to you in that hour; for it is not you who speak but the spirit of your Father speaking through you" (10:19-20).

It is the Spirit who counsels us, but we have to make room for the Spirit, so that he may counsel us. And to give space is to pray, to pray that he comes and help us always.

— General Audience, May 7, 2014

Reflection: To counsel the doubtful is a spiritual work of mercy. What doubts do you have? How can you put aside your own thinking and your own doubts and trust in the counsel of the Lord?

The Church Is Not a Decoration

[At Pentecost] some in Jerusalem would have liked for Jesus' disciples, frozen in fear, to remain locked inside so as not to create confusion. Even today, many would like this from the Christians.... [The Church] doesn't submit to this! She doesn't want to be a decoration. She is a Church that doesn't hesitate to go out, meet the people, proclaim the message that's been entrusted to her, even if that message disturbs or unsettles the conscience, even if that message perhaps brings problems and sometimes leads to martyrdom.

— *Regina Caeli*, June 8, 2014

Reflection: Are you ever afraid to share your faith or state the opinion of the Church to others? Do you avoid doing this because it might offend others, or because they might accuse you of imposing your beliefs on them? Have you ever considered that speaking the truth can be an act of mercy? We must speak in love, but we must also not be held back by fear.

A New Language

The Church born at Pentecost is an astounding community because, with the force of her arrival from God, a new message is proclaimed — the resurrection of Christ — with a new language — the universal one of love....

Thus the Church is called into being forever: capable of astounding while proclaiming to all that Jesus Christ has conquered death, that God's arms are always open, that his patience is always there awaiting us in order to heal us, to forgive us. The risen Jesus bestowed his Spirit on the Church for this very mission.

— *Regina Caeli*, June 8, 2014

Reflection: The mercy given through Jesus' resurrection should breathe new life into us. Is that your experience? Do you have a love that you feel you must share with others? Jesus' mercy changes our sorrow into joy and death into life. With whom can you share this joy?

This Love Changes Our Lives

What is the very first gift of the Holy Spirit? It is the gift of himself, the one who is love and who makes us fall in love with Jesus. And this love changes our lives. That is why we speak of "being born again in the Spirit." It is what Jesus told Nicodemus. You have received the great gift of diversity of charisms, the diversity which becomes harmony in the Holy Spirit, and in service to the Church.

— Address, June 1, 2014

Reflection: Does your love for the Holy Spirit change your life? How is it different? How do you want it to be different? Do you want more joy? Do you want to show more love and mercy to others? Ask God to give you more of the great gift of the Spirit.

Perceive All of His Warmth

[The gift of wisdom] comes from intimacy with God, from the intimate relationship we have with God, from the relationship children have with their Father. And when we have this relationship, the Holy Spirit endows us with the gift of wisdom. When we are in communion with the Lord, the Holy Spirit transfigures our heart and enables it to perceive all of his warmth and predilection.

— General Audience, April 9, 2014

Reflection: Our lives and habits change when we experience the mercy of God more intimately. What's one way that you can have a deeper experience with God this week?

Fear of the Lord

This is why we need this gift of the Holy Spirit so much. Fear of the Lord allows us to be aware that everything comes from grace and that our true strength lies solely in following the Lord Jesus and in allowing the Father to bestow upon us his goodness and his mercy. To open the heart, so that the goodness and mercy of God may come to us.

— General Audience, June 11, 2014

Reflection: How do you open your heart to God? Do you speak to him about your life? Do you take time in silence to allow him to speak?

Earrings, Tattoos, All These Things

I remember once, at the Shrine of Luján, I was in the confessional, where there was a long queue. There was even a very modern young man, with earrings, tattoos, all these things.... And he came to tell me what was happening to him. It was a big and difficult problem. And he said to me: "I told my mother all this, and my mother said to me, go to Our Lady, and she will tell you what you must do." Here is a woman who had the gift of counsel.

— General Audience, May 7, 2014

Reflection: One of the spiritual works of mercy is to counsel the doubtful. Who in your life needs to hear your counsel? What words of mercy do they need to hear? When is the next time you can reach out to them? Ask Mary to guide you.

Welcome the Holy Spirit

When we welcome the Holy Spirit into our hearts and allow him to act, Christ makes himself present in us and takes shape in our lives; through us, it will be he — Christ himself — who prays, forgives, gives hope and consolation, serves the brethren, draws close to the needy and to the least, creates community, and sows peace. Think how important this is: by means of the Holy Spirit, Christ himself comes to do all this among us and for us.

— General Audience, January 29, 2014

Reflection: Do you want to love more ardently? Serve more diligently? Forgive more willingly? The Holy Spirit can allow us to do these things if we open ourselves more to him. Come Holy Spirit, teach us to be like Christ.

True Love Is Boundless

The Holy Spirit, gift of the risen Jesus, conveys divine life to us and thus lets us enter into the dynamism of the Trinity, which is a dynamism of love, of communion, of mutual service, of sharing. A person who loves others for the very joy of love is a reflection of the Trinity. A family in which each person loves and helps one another is a reflection of the Trinity. A parish in which each person loves and shares spiritual and material effects is a reflection of the Trinity.

True love is boundless, but it knows how to limit itself, to interact with others, to respect the freedom of others.

— Angelus, June 15, 2014

Reflection: In the Trinity the Father, Son, and Holy Spirit give themselves to one another freely and completely. We are called to reflect this Trinity in our relationships. Think of two or three friends or acquaintances in your life. Is your love unconditional? Does it reflect trust that the Lord will lead and guide them?

Our Lady of Readiness

FEAST OF THE VISITATION OF THE BLESSED VIRGIN MARY

Today, at the end of the month of Mary, is the feast on which we remember her visit to St. Elizabeth. The Gospel tells us that, after the annunciation of the angel, she went in haste, she lost no time, she went immediately out to serve.

She is the Virgin of readiness, Our Lady of Readiness. She is ready right away to come to our aid when we pray to her, when we ask for her help; her protection is in our favor. In many of life's moments, when we stand in need of her help, her protection, let us remember that she does not make us wait: she is Our Lady of Readiness, she immediately goes to serve.

— Recitation of the Holy Rosary for the Conclusion of the Marian Month of May, May 31, 2014

Reflection: Do you have a readiness to serve like Mary? Do you hope for opportunities to help, or do you avoid serving others and seek comfort? Pray to Mary that you can have a heart like hers, a heart open to giving mercy to others.

Tempted to Give In

Dear friends, sometimes we may be tempted to give in to laziness, or worse, to discouragement, especially when faced with the hardships and trials of life. In these cases, let us not lose heart, let us invoke the Holy Spirit so that through the gift of fortitude he may lift our heart and communicate new strength and enthusiasm to our life and to our following of Jesus.

— General Audience, May 14, 2014

Reflection: What steals your joy in life? What distracts you from being generous? From being motivated? Ask the Holy Spirit to help you to continually seek Jesus' love as a source of your motivation and strength.

A Culture That's Lost Its Memory

A people who don't protect their elderly, who don't take care of their young, are a people without a future, a people without hope. [The] young — the children, the youth — and the old carry history forward. The children, the young, rightly have their biological strength. The elderly offer their memory. But when a community loses its memory, it's over, it's over. It's awful to see a community, a people, a culture that's lost its memory.

— Address to the Sant'Egidio Community, June 15, 2014

Reflection: How do your memories — both good and bad — influence how you live out your faith? What can you learn from the elderly of your community about how their experiences and memories shape their faith? What specific things can you do to help the young people of your parish to value the elderly?

Option for the Poor

The Church has made an option for the poor which is understood as a "special form of primacy in the exercise of Christian charity, to which the whole tradition of the Church bears witness." This option — as [Pope] Benedict XVI has taught — "is implicit in our Christian faith in a God who became poor for us, so as to enrich us with his poverty." This is why I want a Church which is poor and for the poor. They have much to teach us.

— *Evangelii Gaudium*

Reflection: What can poverty teach you? To be grateful for what you have? To be joyful despite your circumstances? Whether you consider yourself financially rich or poor, be poor in heart. Remove your attachments to the things of the world and cling to the love and mercy of God.

The Older Son

Our Father never tires of loving, and his eyes never grow weary of watching the road to his home to see if the son who left and was lost is returning. We can speak of God's hope: our Father expects us always, he doesn't just leave the door open to us, but he awaits us. He is engaged in the waiting for his children. And this Father also does not tire of loving the other son who, though staying at home with him the whole time, does not share in his mercy, in his compassion.

God is not only at the origin of love, but in Jesus Christ he calls us to imitate his own way of loving: "As I have loved you, that you also love one another" (Jn 13:34).

— Homily, March 28, 2014

Reflection: In the story of the Prodigal Son, the older son does not run away like the younger son, and yet he still doesn't share in the mercy of the father. Are there people in your life who need you to wait for them and to be present to them despite their lack of response? Take some time to lift them up in prayer.

Missionary Enterprise

A true missionary ... senses Jesus alive with him in the midst of the missionary enterprise. Unless we see him present at the heart of our missionary commitment, our enthusiasm soon wanes and we are no longer sure of what it is that we are handing on; we lack vigor and passion. A person who is not convinced, enthusiastic, certain, and in love, will convince nobody.

— *Evangelii Gaudium*

Reflection: Are you an enthusiastic witness for Jesus? What holds you back? What robs you of your passion?

In the Battle Against Evil

The main character [in one Gospel story] is a widow whose insistent pleading with a dishonest judge succeeds in obtaining justice from him.... This image of prayer is striking, but let us ask ourselves: Why does God want this? Doesn't he already know what we need? What does it mean to "insist" with God?

This is a good question that makes us examine an important aspect of the faith: God invites us to pray insistently not because he is unaware of our needs or because he is not listening to us. On the contrary, he is always listening, and he knows everything about us lovingly. On our daily journey, especially in times of difficulty, in the battle against the evil that is outside and within us, the Lord is not far away; he is by our side.

— Angelus, October 20, 2013

Reflection: Are there situations or people that you pray for insistently? Have you been at it so long that you think God will never answer? Reflect on the widow in this story and recollect that God is present to you. Be assured that he hears your prayer and is waiting to respond with mercy.

Model of Trust in God

How did Mary live [her] faith? She lived it out in the simplicity of the thousand daily tasks and worries of every mother, such as providing food, clothing, caring for the house.... We can ask ourselves a question: Do we allow ourselves to be illumined by the faith of Mary, who is our Mother? Or do we think of her as distant, as someone too different from us? In moments of difficulty, of trial, of darkness, do we look to her as a model of trust in God who always and only desires our good?

— General Audience, October 23, 2013

Reflection: Mary is our Mother, a mother of mercy. Ask yourself the questions Pope Francis asks above. Ask Mary to help you to have faith as she did.

Message of Hope

Human beings can experience conversion; they must never despair of being able to change their lives. I wish this to be a message of hope and confidence for all, even for those who have committed brutal crimes, for God does not wish the death of the sinner, but that he converts and lives (cf. Ez 18:23).

— World Day of Peace Message, January 1, 2014

Reflection: How does God's mercy give you hope? You may or may not be someone who has committed a crime, but the hope of God's mercy can help you to overcome your sins and failures. Pray with confidence that God continues to hear your prayers. Live with the confidence that he gives you grace to overcome your weaknesses, even when you fall.

The Basis for Restoring Dignity

We cannot ignore the fact that in cities human trafficking, the narcotics trade, the abuse and exploitation of minors, the abandonment of the elderly and infirm, and various forms of corruption and criminal activity take place.... The proclamation of the Gospel will be a basis for restoring the dignity of human life in these contexts, for Jesus desires to pour out an abundance of life upon our cities (cf. Jn 10:10).

— *Evangelii Gaudium*

Reflection: Do you believe that the Gospel is the answer to the many problems of injustice in our world? Do your actions reflect this belief? If not, how can you pray, speak, or act differently?

Even to Those Furthest From Her

The Church that is holy does not reject sinners; she does not reject us all; she does not reject because she calls everyone, welcomes them, is open even to those furthest from her, she calls everyone to allow themselves to be enfolded by the mercy, the tenderness, and the forgiveness of the Father, who offers everyone the possibility of meeting him, of journeying toward sanctity.

— General Audience, October 2, 2013

Reflection: You are the Church. You are called to welcome everyone so that they can receive the love, mercy, and forgiveness of God. Are you open to this call? Are you willing to open your heart more to these possibilities?

Waiting for the Best Moment

He is a patient seeker, our Father! He goes before us, and he waits for us always. He never tires of waiting for us, he is never far from us, but he has the patience to wait for the best moment to meet each one of us. And when the encounter happens, it is never rushed, because God wants to remain at length with us to sustain us, to console us, to give us his joy. God hastens to meet us, but he never rushes to leave us.

— Address, November 23, 2013

Reflection: Bearing wrongs patiently is a spiritual work of mercy and an amazing characteristic of God. How can we emulate God's patience? How might we sustain others, console them, and give joy?

World Day Against Child Labor

[On] June 12, we celebrate the World Day Against Child Labor. Tens of millions of children — did you hear that? — tens of millions are forced to work in degrading conditions, exposed to forms of slavery and exploitation, as well as abuse, maltreatment, and discrimination. I strongly hope that the international community can extend its social protection over minors in order to weaken this scourge of child exploitation....

I invite all of you to pray to Our Lady, who held the Child Jesus in her arms, for these boys and girls who are being exploited through work and also abuse. Hail Mary ...

— General Audience, June 11, 2014

Reflection: It's easy to think about the poor abstractly, but it is important to try to understand their situation and work to change it. Contemplate Our Lady as she held the baby Jesus in her arms. God is calling us to view these children forced into labor with the same reverence. Pray three Hail Marys for them.

All the Days of My Life

Those who celebrate the sacrament [of Marriage] say, "I promise to be true to you, in joy and in sadness, in sickness and in health; I will love you and honor you all the days of my life."... [They say this because] they need Jesus' help to walk beside one another in trust, to accept one another each day, and daily to forgive one another. And this is important! To know how to forgive one another in families because we all make mistakes, all of us!

Address, Pilgrimage of Families, October 26, 2013

Reflection: Are you still holding on to a mistake of a loved one? Maybe they intentionally hurt you. Maybe they made a poor decision that disappointed you. The spiritual works of mercy invite us to forgive all injuries. Call on Jesus for help.

A Step Forward

[The Samaritan Woman] had gone to draw water from the well, but she found another kind of water, the living water of mercy from which gushes forth eternal life. She found the water she had always sought! She runs to the village, that village which had judged her, condemned her, and rejected her, and she announces that she has met the Messiah: the one who has changed her life. Because every encounter with Jesus changes our lives, always. It is a step forward, a step closer to God. And thus every encounter with Jesus changes our life. It is always, always this way.

— Angelus, March 23, 2014

Reflection: When have you encountered Jesus' mercy? How did your life change? Has it continued to change, or have you slid back into old habits? Renew your relationship with God and experience his love once again.

Through Their Physical and Spiritual Sufferings

The Church, too, recognizes the gift that the elderly are for so many communities and parishes. Among the faithful today, they are the mainstay and the majority who attend our liturgical celebrations, who dedicate a great portion of their time to caring for the poor, who visit hospitals and nursing homes, and who are missionaries in vast areas of our continent.

Their prayer has sustained the Church, and their advice has saved more than one priestly or religious vocation. Finally, through their physical and spiritual sufferings, they give us an example of strength and apostolic zeal.

— Homily, Feast of the Presentation of the Lord, February 2, 2008, *Only Love Can Save Us*

Reflection: What elderly members in your community are dedicated to serving the poor? Have you ever asked them why they are so willing to help? Have you ever thanked them for their service?

A Merciful Path

Jesus begins his mission not only from a decentralized place, but also among men whom one would call, refer to, as having a "low profile." When choosing his first disciples and future apostles, he does not turn to the schools of scribes and doctors of the law, but to humble people and simple people, who diligently prepare for the coming of the kingdom of God....

Dear friends, the Lord is calling today, too! The Lord passes through the paths of our daily life.... May each one of you think: the Lord is passing by today; the Lord is watching me; he is looking at me! What is the Lord saying to me? And if one of you feels that the Lord says to you "follow me," be brave, go with the Lord.

— Angelus, January 26, 2014

Reflection: In the Lord's mercy, he has called each one of us to follow him. What path of mercy is he leading you on? Are you willing to follow him?

To Carry Jesus

The Church is not a shop, she is not a humanitarian agency; the Church is not an NGO. The Church is sent to bring Christ and his Gospel to all. She does not bring herself — whether small or great, strong or weak, the Church carries Jesus and should be like Mary when she went to visit Elizabeth. What did Mary take to her? Jesus.

The Church brings Jesus: this is the center of the Church, to carry Jesus! If, as a hypothesis, the Church were not to bring Jesus, she would be a dead Church. The Church must bring Jesus, the love of Jesus, the charity of Jesus.

— General Audience, October 23, 2013

Reflection: Sometimes we can be so caught in our actions, helping the poor, teaching the faith, or caring for the sick, that we forget to bring Jesus. What can you do to bring Jesus with you in all you do, taking Mary as your model?

Strike Up a New Song

You can begin from scratch! Why? Because he is waiting for you, he is close to you, he loves you, he is merciful, he forgives you, he gives you the strength to begin again from scratch! Everybody! And so we are able to open our eyes again, to overcome sadness and mourning to strike up a new song. And this true joy remains even amid trial, even amid suffering, for it is not a superficial joy; because it permeates the depths of the person who entrusts himself to the Lord and confides in him.

— Angelus, December 15, 2013

Reflection: We are our own worst enemies when it comes to our own transformation. Instead of starting from scratch, we continue to let our past haunt us. Instead of working through suffering with joy, we let challenges overcome us with sadness. What part of your life needs a restart? How can you begin again and fight through adversity with joy. Entrust your plan to God.

Headed for a Fall

How much pain is caused in families because one of their members — often a young person — is in thrall to alcohol, drugs, gambling, or pornography! How many people no longer see meaning in life or prospects for the future, how many have lost hope!... If we think we don't need God who reaches out to us through Christ, because we believe we can make do on our own, we are headed for a fall. God alone can truly save and free us.

— Lenten Message 2014

Reflection: In what areas of your life do you try to act apart from God? Where might you be heading for a fall? How can Christ help these situations? Even if all you can do is to make a simple prayer, reach out to the mercy of Christ.

What Does Hatred Come From?

The saints never hated. Understand this well: love is of God, then from whom does hatred come? Hatred does not come from God but from the devil! And the saints removed themselves from the devil; the saints are men and women who have joy in their hearts, and they spread it to others. Never hate, but serve others, the most needy; pray and live in joy. This is the way of holiness!

— Angelus, November 1, 2013

Reflection: The Letter to the Romans tells us, "Let love be genuine; hate what is evil, hold fast to what is good" (12:9-21). Is your love genuine? Is it joyful? Are you able to put away hate from your heart? Find opportunities to serve this week as a way to practice love. Let the mercy of God and the joy that accompanies it be your strength.

As a Father Teaches His Child to Walk

The Prophet Hosea says, "I have walked with you and I taught you how to walk as a father teaches his child to walk" (cf. 11:3). It's beautiful, this image of God! And this is he with us: He teaches us to walk. And it is the same attitude he maintains toward the Church. We, too, despite our resolve to follow the Lord Jesus, experience every day the selfishness and hardness of our heart. When, however, we recognize ourselves as sinners, God fills us with His mercy and with His love.

— General Audience, June 18, 2014

Reflection: Where are you right now in your walk with God? Where is he trying to lead you? Where have you been selfish? We can start our walk again or walk more closely with the Lord when we admit that we are sinners in need of his help and mercy. Renew your walk with him.

To Know Our Own Heart

And we must ask the Lord for two graces. The first: to know what is in our own heart, not to deceive ourselves, not to live in deceit. The second grace: to do what is good in our hearts and not to do the evil that is in our hearts. . . . We must always ask for this grace: to know what is happening in our heart, to constantly make the right choice, the choice for good. And that the Lord help us to love one another.

And if I cannot love another, well, why not? Pray for that person, pray that the Lord make me love him. And like this we move forward, remembering that what taints our lives is the evil that comes from our hearts. And that the Lord can help us.

— Homily, February 16, 2014

Reflection: What is happening in your heart right now? Are you able to make the choice of mercy toward others, especially that person who gets on your nerves or makes life difficult for you? What is God saying to you about this?

Our Deepest Identity

Mission is at once a passion for Jesus and a passion for his people. When we stand before Jesus crucified, we see the depth of his love which exalts and sustains us, but at the same time, unless we are blind, we begin to realize that Jesus' gaze, burning with love, expands to embrace all his people.... He takes us from the midst of his people and he sends us to his people; without this sense of belonging we cannot understand our deepest identity.

— *Evangelii Gaudium*

Reflection: Pope Paul VI said that evangelization is the Church's deepest identity. As members of the Church, this is your deepest identity, too! Meditate on the Cross. See the love and mercy that led Jesus to suffer and die for all people. Ask God to give you this love and mercy, too.

The Closeness He Shows

How good it is for us to contemplate the closeness which [Jesus] shows to everyone! If he speaks to someone, he looks into their eyes with deep love and concern: "Jesus, looking upon him, loved him" (Mk 10:21).

— *Evangelii Gaudium*

Reflection: Evangelization isn't just sharing the faith; it is also how we treat those around us. In your conversations today, concentrate on truly being present with others.

The Priest Will Chastise Me

Someone might say: "But I am afraid that the priest will chastise me." No, the priest will not chastise you. Do you know who you will encounter in the Sacrament of Reconciliation? You will encounter Jesus, who pardons you! Jesus is waiting for you there; and this is a sacrament that makes the whole Church grow.

— General Audience, November 6, 2013

Reflection: Fear so often prevents us from receiving Jesus' mercy. Fear about what others will say. Fear about what others will think. Fear about what we might need to change in our own life. Give these fears to the Lord. Use the sacraments as a source of his mercy to help take your fears away.

Prayer for Our Families

And all families, we need God: all of us! We need his help, his strength, his blessing, his mercy, his forgiveness. And we need simplicity to pray as a family: simplicity is necessary! Praying the Our Father together, around the table, is not something extraordinary: it's easy. And praying the Rosary together as a family is very beautiful and a source of great strength!

And also praying for one another! The husband for his wife, the wife for her husband, both together for their children, the children for their grandparents ... praying for each other. This is what it means to pray in the family, and it is what makes the family strong: prayer.

— Homily, October 27, 2013

Reflection: All of us have different family situations, but in each one we can pray for our family members. Take time to pray an Our Father right now. Ask that each one of your family members can experience God's mercy more deeply.

It Is Not an Easy Journey

In proclaiming the beatitudes, Jesus asks us to follow him and to travel with him along the path of love, the path that alone leads to eternal life. It is not an easy journey, yet the Lord promises us his grace, and he never abandons us.

We face so many challenges in life: poverty, distress, humiliation, the struggle for justice, persecutions, the difficulty of daily conversion, the effort to remain faithful to our call to holiness, and many others. But if we open the door to Jesus and allow him to be part of our lives, if we share our joys and sorrows with him, then we will experience the peace and joy that only God, who is infinite love, can give.

— World Youth Day, April 13, 2014

Reflection: Reflect on your own joys and sorrows. Imagine that Jesus is sitting next to you. Have a conversation with him about them. Ask him to make his mercy more a part of your life.

The Freedom of the Holy Spirit

Closed communities pray to the powers of the earth to help them. And that is not a good path. Let us look to Jesus who sends us to evangelize, to proclaim his name with joy, filled with joy. Let's have no fear of the joy of the Holy Spirit. And never, never let us involve ourselves in things that, in the long run, bring us to become closed in ourselves. In this closedness, there is neither the fruit nor the freedom of the Holy Spirit."

— Homily, *Domus Sanctae Marthae*, April 27, 2013

Reflection: Giving God control over our lives is scary. We want our ways, our preferences, and our desires to remain at the center. Pray that the Holy Spirit would open you to freedom in Christ. With this freedom we will be able to truly share God's mercy with others.

You Know That I Love You

FEAST OF STS. PETER AND PAUL

Peter recovered this trust when Jesus said to him three times: "Feed my sheep" (Jn 21:15-17). Peter thrice confessed his love for Jesus, thus making up for his threefold denial of Christ during the Passion.

Peter still regrets the disappointment which he caused the Lord on the night of his betrayal. Now that the Lord asks him: "Do you love me?" Peter does not trust himself and his own strength, but instead entrusts himself to Jesus and his mercy: "Lord, you know everything; you know that I love you" (Jn 21:17). Precisely at this moment, fear, insecurity, and cowardice dissipate. Peter experienced how God's fidelity is always greater than our acts of infidelity, stronger than our denials.

— Homily, Solemnity of Sts. Peter and Paul,

June 29, 2014

Reflection: What fears, insecurities, and cowardice toward the Lord do you take to prayer? Trust in God's fidelity. Tell him, Lord, you know everything; you know that I love you. Have confidence in his love for you. Trust in his mercy.

The Issue Involves Everyone!

I have always been distressed at the lot of those who are victims of various kinds of human trafficking. How I wish that all of us would hear God's cry: "Where is your brother?" (Gn 4:9). Where is your brother or sister who is enslaved? Where is the brother and sister whom you are killing each day in clandestine warehouses, in rings of prostitution, in children used for begging, in exploiting undocumented labor? Let us not look the other way. There is greater complicity than we think. The issue involves everyone!

— *Evangelii Gaudium*

Reflection: There are almost thirty million people who are slaves in our world today. What impact does this have on you? How can you help? Learn more about this situation from organizations such as International Justice Mission or Catholic Relief Services. Don't ignore the cries of your brothers and sisters.

The Sacraments Spur Us to Be Missionaries

Every encounter with Christ, who in the sacraments gives us salvation, invites us to "go" and communicate to others the salvation that we have been able to see, to touch, to encounter, and to receive, and which is truly credible because it is love.

In this way, the sacraments spur us to be missionaries, and the apostolic commitment to carry the Gospel into every setting, including those most hostile, is the most authentic fruit of an assiduous sacramental life, since it is a participation in the saving initiative of God, who desires salvation for all people.

— General Audience, November 6, 2013

Reflection: What do the sacraments mean to you? Do they lead you to go out to others? Pray for the grace to encounter God's love in the sacraments and to carry this love and mercy to others.

A People With No Future

A people who do not take care of their elderly and their children have no future because they will not have memory and will not have a promise.... The only commandment which brings with it a blessing is the fourth, the commandment which regards honoring our parents and the elderly.

— Homily, *Domus Sanctae Marthae*, September 30, 2013

Reflection: Do you value the elderly? We aren't immune to the pressures and opinions of our culture that often exults youth and dismisses the elderly. How can you see them in light of God's mercy? What can they teach us that no one else can?

New Idols

We have created new idols. The worship of the ancient golden calf (cf. Ex 32:1-35) has returned in a new and ruthless guise in the idolatry of money and the dictatorship of an impersonal economy lacking a truly human purpose. The worldwide crisis affecting finance and the economy lays bare their imbalances and, above all, their lack of real concern for human beings; man is reduced to one of his needs alone: consumption.

— *Evangelii Gaudium*

Reflection: Has money become an idol to you? Where does it have a hold on your heart, your happiness, and your ability to give mercy to others? Where can you use money for the good of others?

A Church of Sinners

You could say to me: But the Church is made up of sinners, we see them every day. And this is true: We are a Church of sinners; and we sinners are called to let ourselves be transformed, renewed, sanctified by God. There has been in history the temptation for some to say: The Church is only the Church of the pure, the perfectly consistent, and expels all the rest. This is not true! This is heresy!

— General Audience, October 2, 2013

Reflection: Do you ever avoid Church or other Christians because of your sins or weaknesses (or theirs)? Reexamine the purpose of Church in light of Pope Francis' words and do not be held back from God's mercy.

Knots That Take Away Our Peace

When children disobey their parents, we can say that a little "knot" is created. This happens if the child acts with an awareness of what he or she is doing, especially if there is a lie involved. At that moment, they break trust with their parents....

Something of the same sort happens in our relationship with God. When we do not listen to him, when we do not follow his will, we do concrete things that demonstrate our lack of trust in him — for that is what sin is — and a kind of knot is created deep within us. These knots take away our peace and serenity. They are dangerous, since many knots can form a tangle which gets more and more painful and difficult to undo.

But we know one thing: nothing is impossible for God's mercy! Even the most tangled knots are loosened by his grace.

— Address, Marian Day, October 12, 2013

Reflection: Do you have knots in your life? Where have you failed to listen to God? What lies have you told to God, or even yourself? Even if the situation may seem hopeless, God's mercy can untangle it. Turn to his mercy again and again as your knots untangle.

Humility, Mercy, and Closeness to Others

[Jesus] is the path! To press forward in faith, to advance in the spiritual pilgrimage which is faith, is nothing other than to follow Jesus; to listen to him and be guided by his words; to see how he acts and to follow in his footsteps; to have his same sentiments.

And what are these sentiments of Jesus? Humility, mercy, closeness to others, but also a firm rejection of hypocrisy, duplicity, and idolatry. The way of Jesus is the way of a love which is faithful to the end, even unto sacrificing one's life; it is the way of the cross.

— Address, Marian Day, October 12, 2013

Reflection: Reflect on the sentiments of Jesus — humility, mercy, and a closeness to others. In which of these areas do you need to grow? Where do hypocrisy, duplicity, and idolatry hold you back?

Beautiful Moments

The life of a family is filled with beautiful moments: rest, meals together, walks in the park or the countryside, visits to grandparents or to a sick person.... But if love is missing, joy is missing, nothing is fun. Jesus always gives us that love: he is its endless source. In the sacrament he gives us his word and he gives us the bread of life, so that our joy may be complete.

— Address, Pilgrimage of Families, October 26, 2013

Reflection: We always have opportunities to serve others within our families. Where do you feel overwhelmed and lack joy as you serve? How can you turn to Jesus in these moments?

The First Step

Being a disciple means being constantly ready to bring the love of Jesus to others.... The first step is personal dialogue, when the other person speaks and shares his or her joys, hopes, and concerns for loved ones, or so many other heartfelt needs. Only afterward is it possible to bring up God's word, perhaps by reading a Bible verse or relating a story, but always keeping in mind the fundamental message: the personal love of God who became man, who gave himself up for us, who is living and who offers us his salvation and his friendship.

— *Evangelii Gaudium*

Reflection: When we think of evangelization, we have to first think of mercy. How can we care for the person with whom we are talking? How can we listen to their joys, hopes, and concerns? Start with mercy in introducing them to our merciful Father.

Small Daily Acts

The Church, guided by the Gospel of mercy and by love for mankind, hears the cry for justice and intends to respond to it with all her might. In this context we can understand Jesus' command to his disciples: "You yourselves give them something to eat!" (Mk 6:37): it means working to eliminate the structural causes of poverty and to promote the integral development of the poor, as well as small daily acts of solidarity in meeting the real needs which we encounter.

— *Evangelii Gaudium*

Reflection: How can you make small acts of solidarity with the poor? What about not wasting any food? How about choosing to not buy something you want, but don't really need? Find ways to think of the poor in your everyday life.

The Tendency to Be Closed and Private

How beautiful it is to support each other in the wonderful adventure of faith! I say this because the tendency to be closed and private has influenced the religious sphere as well, so much so that it often becomes difficult to ask for spiritual help from those who would share this Christian life with us. Who among us has not experienced insecurity, confusion, and even doubt on our journey of faith? We have all experienced this, myself as well. It is part of the journey of faith, it is part of our life. None of this should surprise us, because we are human beings, marked by fragility and limitations.

— General Audience, October 30, 2013

Reflection: Have you experienced the tendency of our society to be more closed off and private? Do you also have this tendency? Find ways to walk with others in their journey of faith. Be open to hearing their stories. Listening is a wonderful act of mercy.

The Christian Meaning of Death

FEAST OF ST. BENEDICT

And so what is the Christian meaning of death? If we look at the most painful moments of our lives, when we have lost a loved one — our parents, a brother, a sister, a spouse, a child, a friend — we realize that even amid the tragedy of loss, even when torn by separation, the conviction arises in the heart that everything cannot be over, that the good given and received has not been pointless. There is a powerful instinct within us which tells us that our lives do not end with death.

This thirst for life found its true and reliable answer in the resurrection of Jesus Christ. Jesus' resurrection does not only give us the certainty of life after death, it also illumines the very mystery of the death of each one of us.

— General Audience, November 27, 2013

Reflection: St. Benedict instructed his monks to "keep death daily before one's eyes" as a means to remind them of what they were living for. If you were to die today, looking back on your life, would you have any regrets about the way you are living? God's mercy is waiting for you. Ask him for forgiveness and resolve to live for him more deeply.

That Is Why Sunday Is So Important to Us

Dear friends, we don't ever thank [the] Lord enough for the gift he has given us in the Eucharist! It is a very great gift, and that is why it is so important to go to Mass on Sunday. Go to Mass not just to pray, but to receive Communion, the bread that is the Body of Jesus Christ who saves us, forgives us, unites us to the Father. It is a beautiful thing to do! And we go to Mass every Sunday because that is the day of the resurrection of the Lord. That is why Sunday is so important to us.

— General Audience, February 5, 2014

Reflection: What does the Eucharist mean to you? How have you experienced God's mercy through this sacrament? Take some time to express your gratitude to God for this great gift.

Contemplate Jesus' Suffering

How can we bear witness? Contemplate Jesus. How can we forgive? Contemplate Jesus' suffering. How can we not hate our neighbor? Contemplate Jesus' suffering. How can we avoid gossiping about our neighbor? Contemplate Jesus' suffering. There is no other way.

— Homily, *Domus Sanctae Marthae*, September 12, 2013

Reflection: Jesus' death on the cross changes everything. He shows us how to take on injustice and how to respond to it. He shows us what love is and how to live it. What does Jesus' suffering show you?

What Dilutes Your Love?

What about us? We who are the Church? What kind of love do we bring to others? Is it the love of Jesus that shares, that forgives, that accompanies, or is it a watered-down love, like wine so diluted that it seems like water? Is it a strong love, or a love so weak that it follows the emotions, that it seeks a return, an interested love?

— General Audience, October 23, 2013

Reflection: What dilutes your love? Self-concern? Fear? Busyness? What keeps you from giving God's mercy more fully to others? What do you need to do in order to strengthen your love?

To Make Us Strong in Life

The sacraments are not decorations in life — what a beautiful marriage, what a beautiful ceremony, what a beautiful banquet.... But that is not the sacrament of marriage. That is a decoration! Grace is not given to decorate life, but rather to make us strong in life, giving us courage to go forward!

— Address, Pilgrimage of Families, October 26, 2013

Reflection: The sacraments are amazing instruments of grace and mercy in our lives. Do you experience them that way? Where do you need strength? Where do you need courage? As you participate in the sacraments, ask God to help you grow in your areas of need.

Are You on the Right Path?

What is the sign that we are on the right path? Scripture tells us: defend the oppressed; take care of your neighbor, the sick, the poor, the needy, the ignorant. This is the touchstone. Hypocrites cannot do this, for they are so full of themselves that they are blind to seeing others. [But] when one journeys a little and draws near to the Lord, the light of the Father enables one to see these things and to go out to help one's brothers and sisters.

— Homily, *Domus Sanctae Marthae*, March 18, 2014

Reflection: What does it mean to be a spiritual hypocrite? Where are you a hypocrite in your own life? How can you get back on the right path?

Loving Attentiveness

Loving attentiveness is the beginning of a true concern for [the poor] which inspires me effectively to seek their good. This entails appreciating the poor in their goodness, in their experience of life, in their culture, and in their ways of living the faith.

True love is always contemplative, and permits us to serve the other not out of necessity or vanity, but rather because he or she is beautiful above and beyond mere appearance.

— *Evangelii Gaudium*

Reflection: What does it mean to practice loving attentiveness? How can you cultivate this virtue in your conversations and in your service to others? How can you do small things with great love?

A Privatized Lifestyle

The Church urgently needs the deep breath of prayer, and, to my great joy, groups devoted to prayer and intercession, the prayerful reading of God's word, and the perpetual adoration of the Eucharist are growing at every level of ecclesial life. Even so ... there is always the risk that some moments of prayer can become an excuse for not offering one's life in mission; a privatized lifestyle can lead Christians to take refuge in some false forms of spirituality.

— *Evangelii Gaudium*

Reflection: Our relationship with God and our relationship with others have a deep connection. We can sometimes fall into the trap of concentrating on loving God and forgetting to love others. Do you ever fall into this trap? How can you get out of it?

Do I Hate Someone?

What is in our heart: is it love? Let us think: do I love my parents, my children, my wife, my husband, people in the neighborhood, the sick?... Do I love? Is there hate? Do I hate someone? Often we find hatred, don't we? "I love everyone except for this one, this one, and that one!" That's hatred, isn't it? What is in my heart, forgiveness? Is there an attitude of forgiveness for those who have offended me, or is there an attitude of revenge — "he will pay for it!" We must ask ourselves what is within, because what is inside comes out and harms, if it is evil; and if it is good, it comes out and does good.

— Homily, February 16, 2014

Reflection: Who is that person in your life you struggle most to love? What needs to change within you so that you can truly love that person? Ask God to help you understand his mercy so that you can give this mercy to others, even those who are the hardest to love.

To Become Saints

Being holy is not a privilege for the few, as if someone had a large inheritance; in baptism we all have an inheritance to be able to become saints. Holiness is a vocation for everyone. Thus we are all called to walk on the path of holiness, and this path has a name and a face: the face of Jesus Christ. He teaches us to become saints.

— Angelus, November 1, 2013

Reflection: Holiness is not about what we can do; it's about what God can do through us. Turn to the face of Jesus. He wants to give you the mercy and grace to become a saint. Trust him and not yourself.

I Always Remember Her

We have received the faith from our fathers, from our ancestors, and they have instructed us in it.... I always remember the face of the nun who taught me the catechism, but she always comes to mind — she is in heaven for sure, because she was a holy woman — I always remember her and give thanks to God for this sister. Or it could be the face of the parish priest, of another priest, or a sister or a catechist, who transmitted the contents of the faith to us and helped us to grow as Christians.

— General Audience, June 25, 2014

Reflection: One of the spiritual works of mercy is to instruct the ignorant. Teaching someone else the faith is one of the greatest opportunities that we have as Christians. Even if you aren't an expert, you still have a great gift to share. Be someone who is remembered years down the road because of your willingness to share your faith with others.

Rediscovering Beauty and Responsibility

Let us rediscover today all the beauty and responsibility of being the Church apostolic! And remember this: The Church is apostolic because we pray — our first duty — and because we proclaim the Gospel by our life and by our words.

— General Audience, October 16, 2013

Reflection: When we proclaim the Gospel by our life and our words, we proclaim God's mercy to others. What aspect of your spiritual life needs work right now — your prayer, your actions, or your words?

Master, Have Mercy on Us!

I think of the ten lepers in the Gospel who were healed by Jesus. They approach him and, keeping their distance, they call out: "Jesus, Master, have mercy on us!" (Lk 17:13). They are sick, they need love and strength, and they are looking for someone to heal them. Jesus responds by freeing them from their disease.

Strikingly, however, only one of them comes back, praising God and thanking him in a loud voice. Jesus notes this: ten asked to be healed and only one returned to praise God in a loud voice and to acknowledge that he is our strength, knowing how to give thanks, to give praise for everything that the Lord has done for us.

— Homily, October 13, 2013

Reflection: What has God done for you? Think back on your own life and the healing that God has granted you. In this time, give thanks to God and allow his past mercy to give you encouragement and faith for the future.

What Does the Mass Do?

When participating in holy Mass, we find ourselves with all sorts of men and women: young people, the elderly, children; poor and well-off; locals and strangers alike; people with their families and people who are alone.... But the Eucharist which I celebrate, does it lead me to truly feel they are all like brothers and sisters? Does it increase my capacity to rejoice with those who are rejoicing and cry with those who are crying? Does it urge me to go out to the poor, the sick, the marginalized? Does it help me to recognize in theirs the face of Jesus?

— General Audience, February 12, 2014

Reflection: The Eucharist is an intimate encounter with God's mercy. Reflect on the Holy Father's questions above. Does this encounter with God's mercy change you so that you are more attuned to the needs of others?

Mercy Triumphs Over Judgment

Feast of St. James

The apostle James teaches that our mercy to others will vindicate us on the day of God's judgment: "So speak and so act as those who are to be judged under the law of liberty. For judgment is without mercy to one who has shown no mercy, yet mercy triumphs over judgment" (Jas 2:12-13).

— *Evangelii Gaudium*

Reflection: Do you struggle with judging others? Perhaps you've made incorrect judgments about the poor, friends, or coworkers. Think through your relationships and the judgments that you have made. How can you replace judgment with mercy?

A Torture Chamber

The confessional must not be a torture chamber, but rather an encounter with the Lord's mercy which spurs us on to do our best. A small step, in the midst of great human limitations, can be more pleasing to God than a life which appears outwardly in order but moves through the day without confronting great difficulties. Everyone needs to be touched by the comfort and attraction of God's saving love, which is mysteriously at work in each person, above and beyond their faults and failings.

— *Evangelii Gaudium*

Reflection: So often we avoid confession because we are weighed down by our sins and limitations. We think: "What does it matter? What difference will it make? I'm no saint." The Lord is willing to help us little by little. Do you have the courage to take the next step?

Craftsmen of Peace

The Spirit allows one to adopt these attitudes [of humility, fraternity, and reconciliation] in daily life, with people of various cultures and religions, and thus to become "craftsmen" of peace. Peace is crafted by hand! There are no industries for peace, no. It is fashioned each day, by hand, and also with an open heart so that the gift of God may come.

— General Audience, May 28, 2014

Reflection: What do you think the relationship between peace and mercy is? Usually we need to practice mercy in order to bring about peace. We need to forgive. We need to love. We need to move on. How can you practice peace this week?

The Depths of Our Existence

Yet a question may stir within us: Is baptism really necessary to live as Christians and follow Jesus? After all, isn't it merely a ritual, a formal act of the Church in order to give a name to the little boy or girl? . . . It is not a formality! It is an act that touches the depths of our existence. A baptized child and an unbaptized child are not the same. A person who is baptized and a person who is not baptized are not the same.

— General Audience, January 8, 2014

Reflection: Do our lives look the same as others who are not baptized? Do we cultivate the mercy and grace given through baptism? If you don't understand the meaning of baptism, read about the sacrament in the Catholic Catechism and consider the ways it can change your life right now.

A Priceless Gift

Jesus' friendship with us, his faithfulness and his mercy, are a priceless gift which encourages us to follow him trustingly, notwithstanding our failures, our mistakes, also our betrayals.... We are all exposed to sin, to evil, to betrayal. We are fully conscious of the disproportion between the grandeur of God's call and of [our] own littleness, between the sublimity of the mission and the reality of our human weakness.

— Address, May 26, 2014

Reflection: What prevents you from trusting in Jesus more fully? Is it your own weaknesses? Is it evil in the world? Turn to Jesus as a friend. Talk to him about where you struggle and why.

Signs to the World

The Gentiles, observing the early Christians, said: how they love each other, how they wish one another well! They do not hate, they do not speak against one another. This is the charity, the love of God that the Holy Spirit puts in our hearts....

Our smallest gesture of love benefits everyone! Therefore, to live out unity in the Church and communion in charity means not seeking one's own interests but sharing the suffering and the joy of one's brothers (cf. 1 Cor 12:26), ready to carry the weight of the poorest and the weakest.

— General Audience, November 6, 2013

Reflection: Sacraments are visible signs, instituted by Christ, to give grace. If we are called to be sacraments of God's love, how can we be visible signs that give grace and mercy to others? What's one way this week you can be a visible sign?

Two Criteria on Love

Feast of St. Ignatius

I am thinking of what St. Ignatius told us.... He pointed out two criteria on love. The first: Love is expressed more clearly in actions than in words. The second: There is greater love in giving than in receiving. These two criteria are like the pillars of true love: deeds, and the gift of self.

— Homily, *Domus Sanctae Marthae*, June 7, 2013

Reflection: So often when we make acts of mercy toward the poor or sick, it is we who receive the most. The Second Vatican Council's document *Lumen Gentium* states, "Man only finds himself through a sincere gift of self." Find opportunities to reach out to others and allow them to help you realize what truly matters in life.

Hypocrites

[When God told Jonah to go to Nineveh to condemn the sin of the people, Jonah fled. This is] the Jonah syndrome ... and Jesus condemns it. For example, in Chapter 23 of Matthew's Gospel, those who have this syndrome are called hypocrites. They do not want the poor to be saved.

The Jonah syndrome afflicts those without zeal for the conversion of others; what they are looking for is a holiness, if I may say, a holiness they can pick up at the dry cleaners. It is clean and pressed, but wholly lacking in the zeal that leads us to preach and proclaim the Lord.

— Homily, *Domus Sanctae Marthae*,
October 14, 2013

Reflection: What do you think of the Holy Father's words? What are some signs that a person might care about holiness, but not about the conversion of others? Do you ever fall into this trap? God's mercy is meant for everyone. Ask the Holy Spirit to give you zeal to share your faith and an openness to be led to do so.

Do I Ask Mary?

Do I ask Mary to help me trust in God's mercy?... She, as a woman of faith, will surely tell you: "Get up, go to the Lord: he understands you." And she leads us by the hand as a mother, our Mother, to the embrace of our Father, the Father of Mercies.

— Address, October 12, 2013

Reflection: Mary knows Jesus so well. She gave birth to him. She lived with him. She journeyed with him, even through his passion, death, and resurrection. Through all of this, Mary remained faithful and accepted God completely into her life. Let her guide you as well.

Is Church Like a Football Match?

Each one of us can ask himself or herself today: How do I live in the Church? When I go to church, is it as though I were at the stadium, at a football match? Is it as though I were at the cinema? No, it is something else. How do I go to church? How do I receive the gifts that the Church offers me to grow and mature as a Christian? Do I participate in the life of the community, or do I go to church and withdraw into my own problems, isolating myself from others?

— General Audience, October 9, 2013

Reflection: In order to experience God's mercy, we have to actively seek to receive it from God and give it to others. Pray about the ways God might want you to get involved in your parish. What active role can you play?

Our Own History

Today we can all think of our own history, our own journey. Each of us has his or her own history: we think of our mistakes, our sins, our good times and our bleak times.

We would do well, each one of us, on this day, to think about our own personal history, to look at Jesus and to keep telling him, sincerely and quietly: "Remember me, Lord, now that you are in your kingdom! Jesus, remember me, because I want to be good, but I just don't have the strength: I am a sinner, I am a sinner. But remember me, Jesus!"

— Homily, November 24, 2013

Reflection: Take some time to think over your own personal history. Look to Jesus and pray the prayer Pope Francis gives us above.

He Gives His Life for People

Jesus is like the Good Samaritan who heals the wounds of life. Jesus is the intercessor who goes away alone to pray for people on the mountain, and he gives his life for people. Jesus wants people to draw close, and he seeks them out; and he is moved when he sees them like sheep without a shepherd. All of this is what the people describe as a new attitude. No, it is not a new teaching, it is a way of making it new.

— Homily, *Domus Sanctae Marthae*,
January 14, 2014

Reflection: Do you have the same attitude as Jesus? Are you willing to make sacrifices to help others grow closer to God? Do you desire to pray for them, to seek them out, to give them mercy?

Our Eyes Are a Little Sick

Purifying the eyes! I am invited to listen to Jesus, and Jesus manifests himself, and by his transfiguration he invites us to gaze at him. And looking at Jesus purifies our eyes and prepares them for eternal life, for the vision of heaven.

Perhaps our eyes are a little sick because we see so many things that are not of Jesus, things that are even against Jesus: worldly things, things that do not benefit the light of the soul. And in this way this light is slowly extinguished, and without knowing it we end up in interior darkness, in spiritual darkness, in a darkened faith: darkness, because we are unaccustomed to looking and imagining the things of Jesus.

— Homily, March 16, 2014

Reflection: What are your eyes fixed on? The things that you watch, what do they tell you about your heart? How can you fix your eyes on Jesus more? Turn your eyes toward his mercy.

God's Ears

The saints are like God's ears — one for each need of his people. We, too, can be saints in a sense. We, too, can be God's ears for our families, in our neighborhoods, where we move about, and where we work. We, too, can be people who listen to the needs of others, not merely to commiserate with them or to go and tell others, but rather to gather together all these needs and present them to the Lord in prayer.

— Homily, Feast of San Cayetano, August 7, 2006,
Only Love Can Save Us

Reflection: How is listening an act of mercy? It is a sacrifice of our time, our desires, and our preferences. Be merciful this week by truly listening to others and presenting their needs to God in prayer.

Restless, Unsettled, Spirit

[St. Peter] Faber was a "modest, sensitive man with a profound inner life. He was endowed with the gift of making friends with people from every walk of life" (Pope Benedict XVI, Address to Jesuits, April 22, 2006). Yet his was also a restless, unsettled, spirit that was never satisfied. . . .

An authentic faith always involves a profound desire to change the world. Here is the question we must ask ourselves: Do we also have great vision and impetus? Are we also daring? Do our dreams fly high? Does zeal consume us (cf. Ps 68:10)?

— Homily to Jesuits, January 3, 2014

Reflection: The mercy the saints received from God drove them to share his love with others. Like St. Peter Faber, are you daring in this endeavor? Does zeal consume you? Ask yourself: Why or why not?

In Peril From Fire

"Maintain constant love for one another, for love covers a multitude of sins" (1 Pt 4:8). This truth greatly influenced the thinking of the Fathers of the Church.... We can recall a single example: If we were in peril from fire, we would certainly run to water in order to extinguish the fire ... in the same way, if a spark of sin flares up from our straw, and we are troubled on that account, whenever we have an opportunity to perform a work of mercy, we should rejoice, as if a fountain opened before [us] so that the fire might be extinguished.

— *Evangelii Gaudium*

Reflection: At times, we can be so focused on the external and material world that we don't take time to consider the spiritual reality around us. Take time to take care of your soul. Acts of mercy help us overcome sin and give us the grace our souls need.

What Prejudices Do You Have?

If we are to share our lives with others and generously give of ourselves, we also have to realize that every person is worthy of our giving. Not for their physical appearance, their abilities, their language, their way of thinking, or for any satisfaction that we might receive, but rather because they are God's handiwork, his creation.

— Evangelii Gaudium

Reflection: What prejudices do you have? Take some time to really think about this. Our prejudices sometimes prevent us from making acts of mercy toward those most in need. Don't let prejudice stop you.

Mercy Over Scorn

The Gospel presents to us the episode of the adulterous woman (cf. Jn 8:1-11), whom Jesus saves from being condemned to death. Jesus' attitude is striking: we do not hear words of scorn, we do not hear words of condemnation, but only words of love, of mercy, which are an invitation to conversion. "Neither do I condemn you; go, and do not sin again" (v. 11).

— Angelus, March 17, 2013

Reflection: Throughout our lives, people will do wrong to us. They will act selfishly. They will say unkind words. What will our response be? Will we be condemning or forgiving? Who has wronged you lately? How can you choose mercy over scorn?

The Anointing of Suffering

Our brothers and sisters who are suffering, who are ill or handicapped, are brothers and sisters anointed by Jesus' own sufferings. They imitate Jesus at the hardest time of his own life, the time of his cross. They endure this anointing of suffering for the sake of the whole Church. Thank you, dear brothers and sisters! Thank you for accepting to be anointed by suffering. Thank you for the hope to which you bear witness, the hope which carries us forward as we seek the caress of Jesus.

— Address, June 1, 2014

Reflection: For the world, suffering is meaningless and should be avoided at all costs. For Christians, suffering is something that can be beautiful and redemptive. What are you suffering from? Unite this suffering to the cross of Christ.

Of Course, It Is Difficult!

With trust in God's faithfulness, everything can be faced responsibly and without fear. Christian spouses are not naive; they know life's problems and temptations. But they are not afraid to be responsible before God and before society. They do not run away, they do not hide, they do not shirk the mission of forming a family and bringing children into the world. But today, Father, it is difficult.... Of course, it is difficult! That is why we need the grace, the grace that comes from the sacrament!

— Address, Pilgrimage of Families,
October 26, 2013

Reflection: Where do you lack courage? When are you tempted to run away from your responsibilities? Ask for God's grace and mercy through the sacraments to help you face your fears and difficulties.

In the Desert

[Pope Benedict the XVI said:] "In the desert, we rediscover the value of what is essential for living; thus in today's world there are innumerable signs, often expressed implicitly or negatively, of the thirst for God, for the ultimate meaning of life. And in the desert, people of faith are needed who, by the example of their own lives, point out the way to the Promised Land and keep hope alive."

— Evangelii Gaudium

Reflection: So often we can mask our real thirsts by distracting ourselves with television, social media, or a variety of different activities. How do you mask your thirst for God and for the ultimate meaning of life? Take a break from these distractions this week. Set aside more time to discover God's love and mercy through prayer, friendships, and the sacraments.

It Makes the World Less Cold

In the past few days I have been reading a book by a cardinal ... on mercy.... Cardinal [Walter] Kasper said that feeling mercy, that this word changes everything. This is the best thing we can feel: it changes the world. A little mercy makes the world less cold and more just. We need to understand properly this mercy of God, this merciful Father who is so patient....

Let us remember the Prophet Isaiah who says that even if our sins were scarlet, God's love would make them white as snow. This mercy is beautiful.

— Angelus, March 17, 2013

Reflection: Do you believe that mercy can change the world? How can it change your area of influence? Make one act of mercy today, no matter how small it may be. Make the world less cold and more just!

Drowning in the Sea of Fears and Anxieties

The Lord in his great goodness and his infinite mercy always takes us by the hand lest we drown in the sea of our fears and anxieties. He is ever at our side; he never abandons us. And so, let us not be overwhelmed by fear or disheartened, but with courage and confidence let us press forward in our journey and in our mission.

— Address, May 26, 2014

Reflection: When faced with challenges in life, it is so easy to forget that Jesus is right by us. Sometimes we don't want to be near him because we are ashamed of our sins or weaknesses. But Jesus wants to be by our side; he wants to be near us. Imagine he's next to you. What do you want to say to him? What is he saying to you?

A Great and Merciful Heart

Let us ask the Lord, each of us, for eyes that know how to see beyond appearance; ears that know how to listen to cries, whispers, and also silence; hands able to support, embrace, and minister. Most of all, let us ask for a great and merciful heart that desires the good and salvation of all.

— Address, May 3, 2014

Reflection: Being merciful often depends on our willingness to be open to God and to be open to those around us. Place yourself in God's presence and ask him to help you do both.

The Blind Man

Our lives are sometimes similar to that of the blind man who opened himself to the light, who opened himself to God, who opened himself to his grace.... I suggest that today, when you return home, you take the Gospel of John and read this passage from Chapter 9. It will do you good, because you will thus see this road from blindness to light and the other evil road that leads to deeper blindness.

Let us ask ourselves about the state of our own heart. Do I have an open heart or a closed heart? It is opened or closed to God? Open or closed to my neighbor? We are always closed to some degree, which comes from original sin, from mistakes, from errors. We need not be afraid! Let us open ourselves to the light of the Lord, he awaits us always in order to enable us to see better, to give us more light, to forgive us.

— Angelus, March 30, 2014

Reflection: As Pope Francis asked his audience, read John 9:1-12. Consider the questions that the Holy Father suggests. Open yourself to the possibilities that come with God's mercy.

Jesus' Work Is Personal

God gets involved with our misery, he draws close to our wounds, and he heals them with his hands; he became man in order to have hands with which to heal us.

Jesus' work is personal: one man committed the sin, one man came to heal it [for] God does not save us merely by decree or by law; he saves us with tenderness, he saves us with caresses, he saves us with his life given for us.

— Homily, *Domus Sanctae Marthae*, October 22, 2013

Reflection: God gets involved with our misery, if we let him. God is willing to heal us, if we reveal our wounds to him. Are you open to his tenderness? Will you let him lead you?

But What Can I Count On?

St. Bernard [says]: But what can I count on? My own merits? No, "my merit is God's mercy. I am by no means lacking merits as long as he is rich in mercy. If the mercies of the Lord are manifold, I too will abound in merits." This is important: the courage to trust in Jesus' mercy, to trust in his patience, to seek refuge always in the wounds of his love.

— Homily, Divine Mercy Sunday, April 7, 2013

Reflection: What do you consider of value in life? What do you hold dear? Do you see that God's mercy is your greatest treasure? Is it more important than your job title, your reputation among friends and family?

We've Always Done It This Way

But [those who are on the outskirts of faith] they are also people and human realities that are marginalized and despised. They are people who perhaps live physically close to the "center" but who spiritually are very far away.... Do not be afraid to go out and meet these people and situations.

Do not allow yourselves to be impeded by prejudice, by habit, by an intellectual or pastoral rigidity, by the famous "we've always done it this way!" However, we can only go to the outskirts if we carry the Word of God in our hearts and if we walk with the Church.

— Address, October 4, 2013

Reflection: How could a perspective of mercy change the way you've always responded to people? Could God be calling you to make a change? To reach out to someone who is different? Ask the Lord for his wisdom.

What Must I Do Now?

Prayer is so important. To pray with the prayers that we all learned as children, but also to pray in our own words. To ask the Lord: "Lord, help me, give me counsel, what must I do now?" And through prayer we make space so that the Spirit may come and help us in that moment, that he may counsel us on what we all must do.

Prayer! Never forget prayer. Never! No one, no one realizes when we pray on the bus, on the road: we pray in the silence of our heart. Let us take advantage of these moments to pray, pray that the Spirit gives us the gift of counsel.

— General Audience, May 7, 2014

Reflection: True mercy can only come through a deeply abiding relationship with Our Lord. Prayer helps us to continually see the world through God's eyes and to ask him how to conform our will with his. Do you pray with your own words? The best way to learn is to try. Take five minutes to speak with Jesus.

Missionary Disciples

Every Christian is challenged, here and now, to be actively engaged in evangelization; indeed, anyone who has truly experienced God's saving love does not need much time or lengthy training to go out and proclaim that love. Every Christian is a missionary to the extent that he or she has encountered the love of God in Christ Jesus: we no longer say that we are "disciples" and "missionaries," but rather that we are always "missionary disciples."

— *Evangelii Gaudium*

Reflection: There are many examples in Scripture of people who experience the mercy of God and then turn to share this mercy with others — the Samaritan woman and St. Paul are two examples. Have you seen this in your own life? How can you more deeply experience the mercy of God so that you can give it to others more richly?

I Am With You Always

To his missionary disciples, Jesus says, "I am with you always, to the close of the age" (Mt 28:20). Alone, without Jesus, we can do nothing! In apostolic work our own strengths, our resources, our structures do not suffice, even if they are necessary. Without the presence of the Lord and the power of his Spirit our work, though it may be well organized, winds up being ineffective.

— *Regina Caeli*, June 1, 2014

Reflection: In the Gospel of John, Jesus tells us that it is good that he leaves this earth because the Holy Spirit will come, and when he does we will do greater works than Jesus did (see 16:7 and 14:12). Invite the Holy Spirit to help you be merciful in your words and in your actions, both here in prayer and throughout the day.

But First in the Heart

Many times, when we examine our conscience, we find some [things] that are truly bad! But [Jesus] carries them. He came for this: to forgive, to make peace in the world, but first in the heart. Perhaps each one of us feels troubled in his heart, perhaps he experiences darkness in his heart, perhaps he feels a little sad over a fault....

He has come to take away all of this. He gives us peace; he forgives everything. "Behold, the Lamb of God, who takes away sin": he takes away sin, its root and all! This is salvation Jesus brings about by his love and his meekness.

— Homily, January 19, 2014

Reflection: Our sins and weakness bring shame, guilt, worry, and fear. Jesus' mercy brings hope, love, and joy. Examine your conscience for a few minutes and consider where you have recently fallen short. Ask God for forgiveness. Free yourself from the bonds of sin. Enter into his mercy.

Our Brothers and Sisters Suffering Today

The season of martyrs is not over. We can truly say that the Church has more martyrs today than she had in the early centuries ... a multitude of men and women who are slandered, persecuted, and killed, in hatred of Jesus, in hatred of the faith. [These] are our brothers and sisters who are suffering today, in this age of martyrs. This must give us food for thought.

— Homily, *Domus Sanctae Marthae*, April 15, 2013

Reflection: What comes to mind when you think about people being martyrs today? How does their sacrifice influence the way you view your own sacrifices? Pray for these martyrs and ask God for the grace to make sacrifices more willingly in your life.

So What Was So New About Jesus?

[The people] were astonished by [Jesus'] teaching, for he taught them as one who had authority, and not as the scribes. [He] taught the Law, he taught Moses and the Prophets. So what was so new? He had power, the power of holiness, unclean spirits fled from him. He was close to sinners, he dined with Matthew, a robber, a traitor to the homeland; he forgave the adulterous woman whom the law would have severely punished; he talked about theology with the Samaritan, who was no "angel," she had her story as well....

[Jesus] looked into people's hearts, Jesus drew near to people's wounded hearts. Jesus was only interested in the person and in God. And he sought to bring God close to people and people close to God.

— Homily, *Domus Sanctae Marthae*,
January 14, 2014

Reflection: Have you ever thought about how powerful Jesus was? Have you ever pictured his miracles in your mind? Have you ever considered how remarkable it is to have the power to take away people's sins and guilt? He still has that same power today, and you have access to it. Trust in the power of his mercy.

Attentive to Mankind Throughout History

The parable of the last judgment is Jesus' way of telling us that God has been attentive to mankind throughout history.... He has been listening every time a beggar has begged — albeit in a low voice that could hardly be heard — and every time one of his children has asked for help.

Moreover, he will be judging us as to whether we have been attentive along with him. He will want to know if we have asked him to hear with his ears in order to know what our brothers and sisters are experiencing so we can help them, or if, on the contrary, we have deafened our ears by putting on earphones so as not to hear anybody.

— Homily, Feast of San Cayetano, August 7, 2006,
Only Love Can Save Us

Reflection: One of the biggest obstacles in the Christian walk is the idea that God is not with us. Since we can't see him, we imagine that he is far away and indifferent. God's mercy extends beyond the cross and into our everyday lives. Tell him what is on your heart and, even more, listen to what he has to say.

Half-Truths or Lies

"When we sin, we have a Paraclete in the Father" [see John 14:16]. And this allows us to breathe. And if we are ashamed? Blessed shame, it is a virtue. The Lord gives us this grace, the courage to walk with him in truth, because the truth is light ... not darkness like half-truths or lies.

— Homily, *Domus Sanctae Marthae*,
April 29, 2013

Reflection: What lies do you tell yourself? What half-truths prevent you from having a richer life in Christ? Turn to God's mercy to find the truth. The truth can be difficult, but it will also give you real freedom and joy.

Confession: A Second Baptism

The Sacrament of Penance, or confession, is, in fact, like a "second baptism" that refers back always to the first to strengthen and renew it.... Think about this: When we go to confess our weaknesses, our sins, we go to ask the pardon of Jesus, but we also go to renew our baptism through his forgiveness. And this is beautiful; it is like celebrating the day of baptism in every confession. Therefore, confession is not a matter of sitting down in a torture chamber, rather it is a celebration.

— General Audience, November 13, 2013

Reflection: Is confession torture for you, or a celebration? Is God's mercy a gift, or something you remain indifferent to? Celebrate confession this week. Let God's mercy help renew you in God's grace.

He Suffers With Us

Jesus is like this: He suffers together with us, he suffers with us, he suffers for us. And the sign of this compassion is the healing of countless people he performed. Jesus teaches us to place the needs of the poor before our own. Our needs, even if legitimate, are not as urgent as those of the poor, who lack the basic necessities of life.... They have no food, they have no clothing, they cannot afford medicine.

— Angelus, August 3, 2014

Reflection: The word compassion comes from the Latin word which means to suffer with. Who are you called to suffer with right now? Who needs your time, your talent, or your resources more than you?

The Most Effective Presentation of the Good News

The poor person, when loved, "is esteemed as of great value," and this is what makes the authentic option for the poor differ from any other ideology, from any attempt to exploit the poor for one's own personal or political interest.

Only on the basis of this real and sincere closeness can we properly accompany the poor on their path of liberation. Only this will ensure that in every Christian community the poor feel at home. Would not this approach be the greatest and most effective presentation of the good news of the Kingdom?

— *Evangelii Gaudium*

Reflection: How can we make our parishes a place where the poor feel at home? Not only the materially poor, but also the spiritually poor — those who struggle with addictions, loneliness, and broken relationships. How can we help them find a path of liberation?

Something New About God

When we live out a spirituality of drawing nearer to others and seeking their welfare, our hearts are opened wide to the Lord's greatest and most beautiful gifts. Whenever we encounter another person in love, we learn something new about God. Whenever our eyes are opened to acknowledge the other, we grow in the light of faith and knowledge of God.

— *Evangelii Gaudium*

Reflection: When you encounter others, do you draw near to them, or do you try to keep your distance? Are you concerned with them or with your next task? Today, try to encounter everyone you meet with love.

People Are Starving

If something should rightly disturb us and trouble our consciences, it is the fact that so many of our brothers and sisters are living without the strength, light, and consolation born of friendship with Jesus Christ, without a community of faith to support them, without meaning and a goal in life.

More than by fear of going astray, my hope is that we will be moved by the fear of remaining shut up within structures which give us a false sense of security, within rules which make us harsh judges, within habits which make us feel safe, while at our door people are starving and Jesus does not tire of saying to us, "Give them something to eat" (Mk 6:37).

— *Evangelii Gaudium*

Reflection: Pope Francis' words call us to reflect on what we truly care about. Do we care more about others simply following rules, or is our deepest desire to see them living with the joy and consolation of a friendship with Jesus? Search your heart and mind for what you truly care about.

The Will to Share

In the Eucharist Jesus does not give just any bread, but the bread of eternal life, he gives himself, offering himself to the Father out of love for us. But we must go to the Eucharist with those sentiments of Jesus, which are compassion and the will to share. One who goes to the Eucharist without having compassion for the needy and without sharing is not at ease with Jesus.

— Angelus, August 3, 2014

Reflection: Is there a relationship between the sacraments and your service to the poor? Do they spur you on to serve others? Does receiving these great gifts of mercy compel you to share this mercy with others? Take time after Mass this week to ask God how he wants you to share his mercy with those in need.

This Magnificent Planet

Who would claim to lock up in a church and silence the message of St. Francis of Assisi or Blessed Teresa of Calcutta? They themselves would have found this unacceptable. An authentic faith — which is never comfortable or completely personal — always involves a deep desire to change the world, to transmit values, to leave this earth somehow better than we found it.

We love this magnificent planet on which God has put us, and we love the human family which dwells here, with all its tragedies and struggles, its hopes and aspirations, its strengths and weaknesses.

— *Evangelii Gaudium*

Reflection: Do you have a heart for God's people? Do you have a desire to change the world? Ask the Lord to increase your love for others, especially those who need to encounter the Lord's mercy amidst their trials and weaknesses.

Our Lady of Help

Mary is able to recognize the traces of God's Spirit in events great and small. She constantly contemplates the mystery of God in our world, in human history, and in our daily lives. She is the woman of prayer and work in Nazareth, and she is also Our Lady of Help, who sets out from her town "with haste" (Lk 1:39) to be of service to others.

— *Evangelii Gaudium*

Reflection: Mary wants to help you and will come to your aide quickly. Ask her to help you see God's Spirit in all of your life's events, great and small. Ask her to help you contemplate God's mercy and remind you of when you can give mercy to others.

I Have Shunned Your Love

Whenever we take a step toward Jesus, we come to realize that he is already there, waiting for us with open arms. Now is the time to say to Jesus: "Lord, I have let myself be deceived; in a thousand ways I have shunned your love, yet here I am once more, to renew my covenant with you. I need you. Save me once again, Lord, take me once more into your redeeming embrace."

— *Evangelii Gaudium*

Reflection: Take some time to recognize that you are in Jesus' presence. Ask him: What step do I need to take to draw closer to you? In what ways have I been deceived, and am in need of your mercy?

Listening

We need to practice the art of listening, which is more than simply hearing. Listening ... is an openness of heart which makes possible that closeness without which genuine spiritual encounter cannot occur. Listening helps us to find the right gesture and word which shows that we are more than simply bystanders.

— *Evangelii Gaudium*

Reflection: Are you good at listening? If we are to receive God's mercy, we must be willing to listen to him and to each other. Take extra time and effort to do both of these this week.

In a Community, in a Family

We cannot grow up by ourselves, we cannot journey on our own, in isolation; rather, we journey and grow in a community, in a family. And so it is in the Church! In the Church we can listen to the Word of God with the assurance that it is the message that the Lord has given us; in the Church we can encounter the Lord in the sacraments, which are the open windows through which the light of God is given to us, streams from which we can draw God's very life; in the Church we learn to live in the communion and love that comes from God.

— General Audience, October 9, 2013

Reflection: With whom do you journey? What influences you the most? Is it the media? Is it your friends? Is it the Lord? Turn to encounters of his mercy to help you center your priorities. Spend time with those who encourage your faith, dive in to God's word, and frequent the sacraments.

The Air of Faith

Let us become bold in exploring new ways with which our communities can be homes where the door is always open. An open door! And it is important that the welcome is followed by a clear proposal of the faith; many times a proposal of the faith may not be explicit but is conveyed by attitude, by witness. In this institution called the Church, in this institution called the parish, one breathes the air of faith, because one believes in the Lord Jesus.

— Address, June 16, 2014

Reflection: How involved are you in your parish? Do you make excuses for why you aren't involved? Your pastor? The people? Your schedule? Find ways to overcome any obstacles and get involved in making your parish a more inviting place that shares the faith.

So Selfish and Proud

The Book of Leviticus says: "You shall not hate your brother in your heart.... You shall not take vengeance or bear any grudge ... but you shall love your neighbor as yourself" (19:17-18). These attitudes are born of the holiness of God. We, however, tend to be so different, so selfish and proud.

— Homily, February 23, 2014

Reflection: One of the spiritual works of mercy is to forgive offenses willingly. Do pride and selfishness prevent you from forgiving others?

With the Eyes of God

And wisdom is precisely this: it is the grace of being able to see every-thing with the eyes of God. It is simply this: it is to see the world, to see situations, circumstances, problems, everything through God's eyes. This is wisdom. Sometimes we see things according to our liking or according to the condition of our heart, with love or with hate, with envy.... No, this is not God's perspective.

— General Audience, April 9, 2014

Reflection: If you saw the world with the eyes of God, how would this change your perspective? How would you be more merciful?

Stealing From the Poor

[St. John Chrysostom once said:] "Not to share one's wealth with the poor is to steal from them and to take away their livelihood. It is not our own goods which we hold, but theirs."...

Money must serve, not rule! The pope loves everyone, rich and poor alike, but he is obliged in the name of Christ to remind all that the rich must help, respect, and promote the poor.

— *Evangelii Gaudium*

Reflection: How does what we do with our money affect our ability to be merciful? How are you called to help, respect, and promote the poor?

Something All of Us Must Do

God's goodness and beauty attract us, and the Holy Spirit is able to purify, transform, and shape us day by day. To make effort to be converted, to experience a heartfelt conversion: this is something that all of us ... must do. Conversion!

— Homily, February 23, 2014

Reflection: How has the Lord changed your heart in the past? How do you think he can change it today? Turn to the Lord's love and mercy and ask him to bring about conversion in your life.

Meeting Jesus

Our whole life is an encounter with Jesus: in prayer, when we go to Mass, and when we do good works, when we visit the sick, when we help the poor, when we think of others, when we are not selfish, when we are loving . . . in these things we always meet Jesus. And the journey of life is precisely this: journeying in order to meet Jesus.

— Homily, December 1, 2013

Reflection: There are so many times in life when we can encounter God's mercy and give his mercy as well. Where have you encountered Jesus this week? What opportunities did you miss? Take time to think about him throughout your day.

Communion Means Common-Union

[In difficult moments,] it is necessary to trust in God's help, through childlike prayer, and, at the same time, it is important to find the courage and the humility to open up to others, to ask for help, to ask for a helping hand. How often have we done this and then succeeded in emerging from our difficulty and finding God again!

In this communion — communion means common-union — we form a great family, where every member is helped and sustained by the others.

— General Audience, October 30, 2013

Reflection: If you have a particular problem, don't hesitate to ask someone for help. Be open to experiencing God's mercy through others. Don't let fear hold you back. Ask them today!

A Little Dead

I would simply like to say something very briefly. We all have within us some areas, some parts of our heart that are not alive, that are a little dead; and some of us have many dead places in our hearts, a true spiritual necrosis! And when we are in this situation, we know it, we want to get out, but we can't. Only the power of Jesus, the power of Jesus can help us come out of these atrophied zones of the heart, these tombs of sin, which we all have.

— Homily, April 6, 2014

Reflection: Do you have a part of your heart that is "a little dead"? Has it caused you to be in a situation that you want to get out of but can't? Have you given this over to Jesus? Do you continue to offer it up to him? Renew your commitment and trust in his power to change you and your circumstance.

Come to Me

Jesus himself sought out these tired, worn out crowds like sheep without a shepherd (cf. Mt 9:35-36), and he sought them out to proclaim to them the kingdom of God and to heal many of them in body and spirit. Now he calls them all to himself: "Come to me," and he promises them relief and rest.

This invitation of Jesus reaches to our day, and extends to the many brothers and sisters oppressed by life's precarious conditions.... In the poorest countries, but also on the outskirts of the richest countries, there are so many weary people, worn out under the unbearable weight of neglect and indifference.

— Angelus, July 6, 2014

Reflection: How can you be Christ to those who are weighed down by heavy burdens? Do you seek these people out or do you wish to avoid their problems? Consider how Jesus seeks you out in your time of need. Take on his attitude of mercy.

No Longer at the Mercy of Evil

We, by baptism, are immersed in that inexhaustible source of life which is the death of Jesus, the greatest act of love in all of history; and thanks to this love we can live a new life, no longer at the mercy of evil, of sin, and of death, but in communion with God and with our brothers and sisters.... Today, at home, go look, ask about the date of your baptism, and that way you will keep in mind that most beautiful day of baptism.

— General Audience, January 8, 2014

Reflection: When we are at the mercy of sin, we are slaves to death, sadness, and fear. But when we receive God's mercy, we receive his life, joy, and courage. Our baptism is a great reminder of the mercy of God. Do you know when you were baptized? Look up the date and mark it on your calendar as the anniversary of your new life in Christ.

Simple, Humble Hearts

In the Gospel [Jesus] shows us the way, the way of the Beatitudes (cf. Mt 5:1-12). In fact, the kingdom of heaven is for those who do not place their security in material things but in love for God, for those who have a simple, humble heart that does not presume to be just and does not judge others, for those who know how to suffer with those who suffer and how to rejoice when others rejoice.

They are not violent but merciful and strive to be instruments for reconciliation and peace.

— Angelus, November 1, 2013

Reflection: Read the Gospel of Matthew 5:1-12. Ask God for a simple humble heart that seeks justice and mercy and to suffer and to rejoice with others.

The Culture of Well-Being

Each and every one of us needs to examine our conscience and find out what riches keep us from approaching Jesus on the road of life. [The first is] well-being or [comfort]. The culture of well-being that gives us little courage, makes us lazy and selfish.

— Homily, *Domus Sanctae Marthae*, May 27, 2013

Reflection: A culture of well-being can cause us to seek comfort and to avoid others. Where does this attitude creep up in your own life? What do you need to do to prevent yourself from going down this path?

Close to Jesus

How do we stay close to Jesus? Through prayer, in the sacraments, and also in the exercise of charity. Let us remember that he is present in the weakest and the most needy.

— General Audience, November 27, 2013

Reflection: Pope Francis asks us how we stay close to Jesus. Ask yourself, though, if you really want to stay close. Does Jesus make you uncomfortable? Do you have trouble believing he hears you? Resolve this week — through prayer, the sacraments, and acts of charity — to invite him more deeply into your life, and then pay attention to those moments when he might be quietly drawing you closer to him.

Don't Cage the Holy Spirit

Go out into the streets and evangelize. Proclaim the Gospel. Remember that the Church was born "on the move" that Pentecost morning. Draw close to the poor and touch in their flesh the wounded flesh of Jesus. Let yourselves be guided by the Holy Spirit, in freedom; and please, don't put the Holy Spirit in a cage! Be free!

— Address, June 1, 2014

Reflection: Life in the Spirit is a life that is ready to hear God's call and to move in the direction that he points. Are you open to his call? Do you have freedom in the Spirit, or are you caged by your selfishness?

The Restlessness of the Search

Because we are sinners, we can ask ourselves if our heart has preserved the restlessness of the search or if instead it has atrophied; if our heart is always in tension: a heart that does not rest, that does not close in on itself but beats to the rhythm of a journey undertaken together with all the people faithful to God. We need to seek God in order to find him, and find him in order to seek him again and always.

— Homily to Jesuits, January 3, 2014

Reflection: Do you continue to seek God's mercy, or have you given up? It can be easy to give up, but when we seek him, we get back on track. In seeking him we receive grace to seek him further. Talk with God about continuing on this path. Don't give up!

We Go Forward

I go to my brother priest and I say: "Father, I did this ..." And he responds: "But I forgive you; God forgives you." At that moment, I am sure that God has forgiven me! And this is beautiful, this is having the surety that God forgives us always, he never tires of forgiving us.

And we must never tire of going to ask for forgiveness. You may feel ashamed to tell your sins, but as our mothers and our grandmothers used to say, it is better to be red once than yellow a thousand times. We blush once, but then our sins are forgiven and we go forward.

— General Audience, November 20, 2013

Reflection: When's the last time you went to confession? Even a holy person like the pope makes time to confess his sin. Confession will help you become a better version of yourself. Go, and then move forward!

Crafters of Peace

The world has much need of us as messengers of peace, witnesses of peace! The world needs this. The world asks us to bring peace and to be a sign of peace!

Peace is not something which can be bought or sold; peace is a gift to be sought patiently and to be "crafted" through the actions, great and small, of our everyday lives. The way of peace is strengthened if we realize that we are all of the same stock and members of the one human family; if we never forget that we have the same Father in heaven and that we are all his children, made in his image and likeness.

— Homily, Pilgrimage to the Holy Land, May 24, 2014

Reflection: How can you be a crafter of peace and mercy? Who are you having differences with right now? Consider how you can bring about peace in this situation.

Do We Just Tend Our Own Vegetable Patch?

FEAST OF ST. VINCENT DE PAUL

Is self-interested love pleasing to Jesus? No, it is not, because love should be freely given, like his is. What are the relationships like in our parishes, in our communities? Do we treat each other like brothers and sisters? Or do we judge one another, do we speak evil of one another, do we just tend our own vegetable patch? Or do we care for one another? These are the questions of charity!

— General Audience, October 23, 2013

Reflection: St. Vincent de Paul once said: "Extend your mercy toward others, so that there can be no one in need whom you meet without helping. For what hope is there for us if God should withdraw his mercy from us?" Consider the questions from Pope Francis above. Which people in your life need to receive your mercy?

The Knots of Our Soul

FEAST OF MARY UNDOER OF KNOTS

Mary, whose "yes" opened the door for God to undo the knot of the ancient disobedience, is the Mother who patiently and lovingly brings us to God, so that he can untangle the knots of our soul by his fatherly mercy.

We all have some of these knots, and we can ask in our heart of hearts: What are the knots in my life? "Father, my knots cannot be undone!" It is a mistake to say anything of the sort! All the knots of our heart, every knot of our conscience, can be undone.

— Address, October 12, 2013

Reflection: What knots do you have in your life? Which of these have built up over time and weakened your relationship with God? Pope Francis has a special devotion to Mary, Undoer of Knots. Look up a novena to her and pray it over the next nine days for your intention. Pray that God's mercy will help undo your knot.

He Opens Hearts

This is what the Holy Spirit does through the gift of fear of the Lord: he opens hearts. The heart opens so that forgiveness, mercy, goodness, and the caress of the Father may come to us, for as children we are infinitely loved.

— General Audience, June 11, 2014

Reflection: One of the seven gifts of the Holy Spirit is fear of the Lord. We don't fear God because he might punish us. Rather, we fear that we will disappoint God as a child disappoints his father. Pray for this gift of the Spirit. It allows us as sons and daughters to ask for his help and to readily accept his love and mercy.

The Work of His Mercy

The salvation which God offers us is the work of his mercy. No human efforts, however good they may be, can enable us to merit so great a gift. God, by his sheer grace, draws us to himself and makes us one with him. He sends his Spirit into our hearts to make us his children, transforming us, and enabling us to respond to his love by our lives.

— *Evangelii Gaudium*

Reflection: God draws near to us with his mercy first, before we can do anything. And his Holy Spirit enables us to respond to his love. Have you invited his Spirit into your life? Open your heart and allow his Spirit to transform you.

Raise Your Hand

FEAST OF ST. THÉRÈSE OF LISIEUX

In life we err frequently, we make many mistakes. We all do. Wait, maybe someone here has never made a mistake? Raise your hand if you are that someone, there: a person who has never made a mistake? We all do it! All of us! Perhaps not a day goes by without making some mistake.... Let us learn to acknowledge our mistakes and to ask for forgiveness.

— Address to Engaged Couples, February 14, 2014

Reflection: St. Thérèse of Lisieux once said, "How happy I am to see myself imperfect and be in need of God's mercy." It can be difficult to accept our mistakes, but it gives us an opportunity to see God's mercy and to rely on it more deeply. When you make a mistake today, take the opportunity to pray for a greater reliance on God's mercy.

Who Is Helping and Who Is Being Helped?

You have also learned to see others, particularly *the poor*; and I hope you … don't distinguish between who is helping and who is being helped. The tension slowly ceases being tension and becomes an encounter, an embrace: it becomes unclear who helps and who is being helped. Who leads the action? Both of them, or, to say it better, the embrace leads.

— Address to the Sant'Egidio Community,
June 15, 2014

Reflection: When you think of helping the poor do you think that they are also helping you? When we help the poor, we become better versions of ourselves. We learn to be less selfish, less comfortable, and more loving. Embrace this encounter.

Mercy and New Strength

When we are weary, downcast, beset with cares, let us look to Mary, let us feel her gaze, which speaks to our heart and says, "Courage, my child, I am here to help you!" Our Lady knows us well, she is a mother, she is familiar with our joys and difficulties, our hopes and disappointments.

When we feel the burden of our failings and our sins, let us look to Mary, who speaks to our hearts, saying, "Arise, go to my Son, Jesus; in him you will find acceptance, mercy, and new strength for the journey."

— Message, October 12, 2013

Reflection: Mary is our guide to accepting Jesus into our life in deeper and more profound ways. Take your current difficulties and disappointments and bring them to Mary to help you grow closer to Our Lord.

The Leper Changed St. Francis

FEAST OF ST. FRANCIS

St. Francis was a rich young man, he had ideals of glory, but Jesus, in the person of a leper, spoke to him in silence, and he changed him, he made him understand what truly mattered in life: not wealth, nor power of weapons, nor earthly glory, but humility, mercy, and forgiveness.

— Address, Meeting with Sick and Disabled
Children, October 4, 2013

Reflection: Reflect on what matters to you in life. Use the silence and allow God to speak to you about your priorities. Where do humility, mercy, and forgiveness rank?

An Abyss Beyond Our Comprehension

FEAST OF ST. FAUSTINA

It is not easy to entrust oneself to God's mercy, because it is an abyss beyond our comprehension. But we must!... "Oh, I am a great sinner!" All the better! Go to Jesus: He likes you to tell him these things! He forgets; he has a very special capacity for forgetting. He forgets, he kisses you, he embraces you, and he simply says to you, "Neither do I condemn you; go, and sin no more" (Jn 8:11).

— Homily, March 17, 2013

Reflection: St. Faustina wrote this message from Jesus in her diary: "Know, my daughter, that between me and you there is a bottomless abyss, an abyss which separates the Creator from the creature. But this abyss is filled with my mercy." Contemplate this abyss and the loving mercy that Jesus offers as he forgives and loves us.

I Am Angry With This Person

We all have our likes and dislikes, and perhaps at this very moment we are angry with someone. At least let us say to the Lord: "Lord, I am angry with this person, with that person. I pray to you for him and for her." To pray for a person with whom I am irritated is a beautiful step forward in love, and an act of evangelization. Let us do it today!

— *Evangelii Gaudium*

Reflection: One of the spiritual works of mercy is to pray for others. Prayer is a powerful act of mercy, both for the person for whom we pray and for ourselves. Today, pray a Chaplet of Divine Mercy for someone who irritates you.

The Breath of Faith

FEAST OF OUR LADY OF THE ROSARY

Prayer is the breath of faith: in a relationship of trust, in a relationship of love, dialogue cannot be left out, and prayer is the dialogue of the soul with God. October is also the month of the Rosary, and on this first Sunday it is tradition to recite the Prayer to Our Lady of Pompeii, the Blessed Virgin Mary of the Most Holy Rosary.

Let us join spiritually together in this act of trust in our Mother, and let us receive from her hands the crown of the Rosary: The Rosary is a school of prayer, the Rosary is a school of faith!

— Angelus, October 6, 2013

Reflection: Look up and recite the Prayer of Our Lady of Pompeii. In this month of the Rosary, make a resolution to pray the Rosary, whether once this month, once a week, or even once a day.

The Reality That Does Not Perish

The Eucharist communicates the Lord's love for us: a love so great that it nourishes us with himself; a freely given love, always available to every person who hungers and needs to regenerate his own strength. To live the experience of faith means to allow oneself to be nourished by the Lord and to build one's own existence not with material goods but with the reality that does not perish: the gifts of God, his Word and his Body.

— Homily, June 19, 2014

Reflection: The Eucharist is a great reminder of how much the Lord seeks to be near us. He wants to make his love tangible to us. He wants to give us life. Arrive at Mass early this week. Prepare yourself for this great gift of God's tremendous mercy. Don't take it for granted.

Thank You, Sorry, Excuse Me

Saying "thank you" is such an easy thing, and yet so hard! How often do we say "thank you" to one another in our families? These are essential words for our life in common. "Sorry," "excuse me," "thank you." If families can say these three things, they will be fine. "Sorry," "excuse me," "thank you." How often do we say "thank you" in our families? How often do we say "thank you" to those who help us, those close to us, those at our side throughout life? All too often we take everything for granted! This happens with God, too.

— Homily, October 13, 2013

Reflection: The words sorry, excuse me, and thank you are words that can help you be merciful or receive mercy from others. Who needs to hear you say "sorry," "excuse me," and "thank you"? In what areas of your life do you need to say these things to God?

An Endless Desire to Show Mercy

The Church which "goes forth" is a community of missionary disciples who take the first step, who are involved and supportive, who bear fruit and rejoice.

An evangelizing community knows that the Lord has taken the initiative, he has loved us first (cf. 1 Jn 4:19), and therefore we can move forward, boldly take the initiative, go out to others, seek those who have fallen away, stand at the crossroads, and welcome the outcast. Such a community has an endless desire to show mercy, the fruit of its own experience of the power of the Father's infinite mercy.

— *Evangelii Gaudium*

Reflection: Have you ever had someone take the initiative in loving and welcoming you? What did it feel like? How did it change you? Where can you boldly take initiative?

He Wasted All the Money

Let us recall that beautiful, beautiful parable of the son who left his home with the money of his inheritance. He wasted all the money and then, when he had nothing left, he decided to return home, not as a son but as a servant. His heart was filled with so much guilt and shame. The surprise came when he began to speak, to ask for forgiveness; his father did not let him speak, he embraced him, he kissed him, and he began to make merry. But I am telling you: Each time we go to confession, God embraces us. God rejoices!

— General Audience, February 19, 2014

Reflection: Do you have guilt and shame in your life right now? Are you afraid of what God thinks of you? Consider the story of the Prodigal Son (also called the story of the Merciful Father). God is waiting to embrace you, not condemn you.

The Way We See the Poor

All of us need to experience a conversion in the way we see the poor. We have to care for them and be sensitive to their spiritual and material needs. To you young people I especially entrust the task of restoring solidarity to the heart of human culture. Faced with old and new forms of poverty — unemployment, migration, and addictions of various kinds — we have the duty to be alert and thoughtful, avoiding the temptation to remain indifferent.

— World Youth Day Message, April 13, 2014

Reflection: In what ways do you need to experience conversion in regard to the poor? Do you remain indifferent to their needs? How can mercy change your perspective? How can it make you more attentive, more caring, more open to helping others?

So Very Merciful

[In the story of the Samaritan woman] the Gospel says that the disciples marveled that their Master was speaking to this woman. But the Lord is greater than prejudice, which is why he was not afraid to address the Samaritan woman; mercy is greater than prejudice. We must learn this well! Mercy is greater than prejudice, and Jesus is so very merciful, very!

— Angelus, March 23, 2014

Reflection: In this story, the disciples marvel at their Master. Do you ever marvel at your Master? What characteristics do you value about Jesus? How have these affected your life? How can you take on these characteristics yourself?

The Sulfur Will Kill You

It is very hard to cut ties with a sinful situation. It is hard!... But the voice of God tells us this word: Flee! You cannot fight here, because the fire, the sulfur will kill you. Flee!

— Homily, *Domus Sanctae Marthae*, July 2, 2013

Reflection: God's mercy can sometimes be an abstract idea or a nice concept. But when we face hardships and temptations, God's mercy can become real and tangible. We experience his mercy when he gives us the strength to flee from what is wrong and cling to what is right. Have you experienced this before? Are you experiencing this right now?

Let Us Imitate Jesus

Let us imitate Jesus: He goes to the streets, not planning for the poor or the sick or disabled people that he crosses along the way; but with the first one he encounters, he stops, becoming a presence of care, a sign of the closeness of God who is goodness, providence, and love.

— Address, June 14, 2014

Reflection: Are you willing to stop what you are doing in order to help others? Are you open to random acts of mercy no matter how small they might be? Imitate Jesus' willingness to be interrupted.

Little by Little

In intimacy with God and in listening to his Word, little by little we put aside our own way of thinking, which is most often dictated by our closures, by our prejudice, and by our ambitions, and we learn instead to ask the Lord: What is your desire? What is your will? What pleases you?

— General Audience, May 7, 2014

Reflection: In order to practice mercy, we must be open to the will of the Father and the guidance of the Holy Spirit. Just like Pope Francis suggests, ask the Lord: What is your desire? What is your will? What pleases you?

A Clear Mandate, Not Just an Option!

Jesus' last message to his disciples is the mandate to depart: "Go, therefore, and make disciples of all nations" (Mt 28:19). It is a clear mandate, not just an option! The Christian community is a community "going forth," "in departure." More so: the Church was born "going forth." And you will say to me: What about cloistered communities? Yes, these too, for they are always "going forth" through prayer, with the heart open to the world, to the horizons of God. And the elderly, the sick? They, too, through prayer and union with the wounds of Jesus.

— *Regina Caeli*, June 1, 2014

Reflection: Each of us is called to be an instrument of God's mercy in this world. How can you pray for others? What words can you speak to convey God's mercy? What merciful actions can you take? In all things, unite yourself to Jesus' sacrifice on the cross.

God Remembers

There is no profession or social condition, no sin or crime of any kind that can erase from the memory and the heart of God even one of his children. God remembers, always, he never forgets those who he created. He is the Father, who watchfully and lovingly waits to see the desire to return home be reborn in the hearts of his children. And when he sees this desire, even simply hinted at and so often almost unconsciously, immediately he is there, and by his forgiveness he lightens the path of conversion and return.

— Angelus, November 3, 2013

Reflection: What separates you from God? So often we think the separation is due to our sins or weaknesses, but in reality it is often because of our unwillingness to ask for forgiveness or to beg God for his grace and mercy. Take a moment to place your sins and weaknesses in his hands.

The Leftovers

Human beings are themselves considered consumer goods to be used and then discarded. We have created a "throw away" culture which is now spreading. It is no longer simply about exploitation and oppression, but something new. Exclusion ultimately has to do with what it means to be a part of the society in which we live; those excluded are no longer society's underside, or its fringes, or its disenfranchised — they are no longer even a part of it. The excluded are not the "exploited" but the outcast, the "leftovers."

— Evangelii Gaudium

Reflection: Who is excluded in your community, your parish, your workplace, or your family? Who needs mercy? Reach out to that person this week.

The Only Real Sadness in Life

There is a celebrated saying by the French writer Léon Bloy, who in the last moments of his life said, "The only real sadness in life is not becoming a saint." Let us not lose the hope of holiness; let us follow this path. Do we want to be saints? The Lord awaits us, with open arms.

— General Audience, October 2, 2013

Reflection: When we think of the idea of becoming a saint, we are quickly overwhelmed by what we must do and how we must change. We must act, yes, but first we must open ourselves up to God's mercy. His mercy is what will change us into saints. Take some time to give yourself to the Lord with open arms.

Our Real Journey

Even if we are sometimes unfaithful to him, he remains faithful. In his mercy, he never tires of stretching out his hand to lift us up, to encourage us to continue our journey, to come back and tell him of our weakness, so that he can grant us his strength. This is the real journey: to walk with the Lord always, even at moments of weakness, even in our sins. Never to prefer a makeshift path of our own. That kills us.

— Homily, October 13, 2013

Reflection: What journey is the Lord leading you on? Where have you left the path? In his mercy, Jesus stretches his hand toward you. Ask God for the courage and strength to reach out to him.

Grace: A Gift From God

We need that sense of gratuitousness [of time and affection freely given]: in families, in parishes, and in society as a whole. And when we think of how the Lord is revealed to us through the free gift, that is, grace, it's a much more important thing.... But if we don't have a sense of gratuitousness in the family, at school, in the parish, it will be very difficult for us to understand what the grace of God is, the grace that isn't sold, that isn't bought, but a present, a gift from God: it is God himself.

— Address, June 14, 2014

Reflection: Do you leave time in your day and in your heart for the gratuitousness that Pope Francis is talking about? Are you able to go the extra mile for those in your family and community? Turn to God's grace as a source of inspiration and strength.

His Way of Life

Jesus' whole life, his way of dealing with the poor, his actions, his integrity, his simple daily acts of generosity, and finally his complete self-giving, is precious and reveals the mystery of his divine life. Whenever we encounter this anew, we become convinced that it is exactly what others need, even though they may not recognize it: "What therefore you worship as unknown, this I proclaim to you" (Acts 17:23).

— *Evangelii Gaudium*

Reflection: This next month commit to reading one of the Gospels, little by little, each day. Reflect on Jesus' every action and intention. Witness his mercy and ask yourself how you can live out his example in your everyday life.

Spirit-filled Evangelizers

Spirit-filled evangelizers are evangelizers who pray and work.... Without prolonged moments of adoration, of prayerful encounter with the word, of sincere conversation with the Lord, our work easily becomes meaningless; we lose energy as a result of weariness and difficulties, and our fervor dies out.

— *Evangelii Gaudium*

Reflection: We can't give what we don't have. If we don't have an ongoing relationship with God and the mercy he provides, how can we expect to be merciful? Be resolved to set aside time each day just to pray and to find moments during the day to lift your heart up to God.

God Never Ceases to Remember You

And I say to you: If your conscience is weighed down, if you are ashamed of many things that you have done, stop for a moment, do not be afraid. Think about the fact that someone is waiting for you because he has never ceased to remember you; and this someone is your Father, it is God who is waiting for you!... I assure you that you will not be disappointed. Jesus is merciful and never grows tired of forgiving! Remember that this is the way Jesus is.

— Angelus, November 3, 2013

Reflection: When you think of Jesus, what comes to mind? Is he angry with you? Condemning? What about merciful? Where in your life do you need to seek forgiveness?

How Is This Possible?

[The apostle Paul wrote:] "Put on then, as God's chosen ones, holy and beloved, compassion, kindness, lowliness, meekness, and patience, forbearing one another and, if one has a complaint against another, forgiving each other; as the Lord has forgiven you, so you also must forgive" (cf. Col 3:12-14).

But how is this possible? How can I prepare myself for this? What do I have to study. The answer is clear: With our own strength, we cannot do it. Grace alone can do it in us. Our effort helps; it's necessary, but not enough."

— Homily, *Domus Sanctae Marthae*, September 12, 2013

Reflection: Which characteristic do you need to put on? Compassion, kindness, lowliness, meekness, or patience? Ask God for his grace to help you change and be open to opportunities to make a step in the right direction this week.

Authentic Prayer

The Gospel passage [Lk 18:9-14] speaks about two ways of praying, one is false — that of the Pharisee — and the other is authentic — that of the tax collector. The Pharisee embodies an attitude which does not express thanksgiving to God for his blessings and his mercy, but rather self-satisfaction. The Pharisee feels himself justified, he feels his life is in order, he boasts of this, and he judges others from his pedestal.

The tax collector, on the other hand, does not multiply words. His prayer is humble, sober, pervaded by a consciousness of his own unworthiness, of his own needs. Here is a man who truly realizes that he needs God's forgiveness and his mercy.

— Homily, October 27, 2013

Reflection: What does it mean for your prayer to be authentic? How can your prayer be humble, sober, and filled with gratitude? Take some time to make a simple and authentic prayer to God. Include the ways in which you are thankful and where you need help.

People's Thirst for God

Today, our challenge is not so much atheism as the need to respond adequately to many people's thirst for God, lest they try to satisfy it with alienating solutions or with a disembodied Jesus who demands nothing of us with regard to others. Unless these people find in the Church a spirituality which can offer healing and liberation, and fill them with life and peace, while at the same time summoning them to fraternal communion and missionary fruitfulness, they will end up by being taken in by solutions which neither make life truly human nor give glory to God.

— *Evangelii Gaudium*

Reflection: Do you know any atheists? How do you think they will find healing and liberation? God has placed you in their lives for a reason. Help them see how God's mercy has changed your life.

Do Not Watch Life Go by From the Balcony!

Whoever does not face challenges, whoever does not take up challenges, is not living. Your willingness and your abilities, combined with the power of the Holy Spirit who abides in each of us from the day of baptism, allow you to be more than mere spectators, they allow you to be protagonists in contemporary events.

Please do not watch life go by from the balcony! Mingle where the challenges are calling you to help carry life and development forward, in the struggle over human dignity, in the fight against poverty, in the battle for values, and in the many battles we encounter each day.

— Homily, November 30, 2013

Reflection: What challenges are you facing right now? Are you a mere spectator? Or are you moving forward? Ask God for the strength to help you overcome what you are facing. Turn to his mercy and receive his strength throughout the day when faced with your trials.

That Your Joy May Be Complete

Dear families, the Lord knows our struggles: he knows them. He knows the burdens we have in our lives. But the Lord also knows our great desire to find joy and rest! Do you remember? Jesus said, "... that your joy may be complete" (cf. Jn 15:11). Jesus wants our joy to be complete! He said this to the apostles, and today he says it to us.

— Address, Pilgrimage of Families, October 26, 2013

Reflection: Take some time to think about all of your family members. Jesus wants each to be happy and to receive his mercy. Pray to God on their behalf, that they might come to know him more deeply so that their joy may be complete.

Plunged Into the Deep

It is true that ... trust in the unseen can cause us to feel disoriented: it is like being plunged into the deep and not knowing what we will find. I myself have frequently experienced this. Yet there is no greater freedom than that of allowing oneself to be guided by the Holy Spirit, renouncing the attempt to plan and control everything to the last detail, and instead letting him enlighten, guide, and direct us, leading us wherever he wills.

The Holy Spirit knows well what is needed in every time and place. This is what it means to be mysteriously fruitful!

— *Evangelii Gaudium*

Reflection: Trusting in God's mercy means giving ourselves over to a God who knows what's best for us. Where do you struggle with giving over control? Give this area over to God and trust that he will guide and direct you.

This Is the Life of a Saint

FEAST OF ALL SAINTS

The saints are not supermen, nor were they born perfect. They are like us, like each one of us. They are people who, before reaching the glory of heaven, lived normal lives with joys and sorrows, struggles and hopes. What changed their lives? When they recognized God's love, they followed it with all their heart without reserve or hypocrisy. They spent their lives serving others, they endured suffering and adversity without hatred and responded to evil with good, spreading joy and peace. This is the life of a saint.

— Angelus, November 1, 2013

Reflection: Do you find it hard to relate to the saints? So often we only read or hear about their accomplishments and not their struggles. Read about St. Gianna Molla or Blessed Pier Giorgio for insight into how they overcame sin and weaknesses by relying on God's grace.

What Will My Passing Away Be Like?

FEAST OF ALL SOULS

Today, before evening falls, each one of us can think of the twilight of life: "What will my passing away be like?" All of us will experience sundown, all of us! Do we look at it with hope? Do we look with that joy at being welcomed by the Lord? This is a Christian thought that gives us hope. Today is a day of joy; however, it is serene and tranquil joy, a peaceful joy.

— Homily, November 1, 2013

Reflection: Praying for the living and the dead is one of the spiritual works of mercy. Take some time to pray for those who have died, and consider your own death. Is your perspective toward death one of hope or dread?

Where Is My Heart Anchored?

Let us think about the passing away of so many of our brothers and sisters who have preceded us, let us think about the evening of our life, when it will come. And let us think about our hearts and ask ourselves: "Where is my heart anchored?" If it is not firmly anchored, let us anchor it beyond, on that shore, knowing that hope does not disappoint because the Lord Jesus does not disappoint.

— Homily, November 1, 2013

Reflection: Are our lives anchored in the hope of mercy that comes with the Resurrection? Do we live our lives as if this is true? Consider where your hope lies and re-anchor your life in Christ if you have found that you have been drifting away.

Together With Mary

Together let us pray to the Virgin Mary, that she helps us ... to walk in faith and charity, ever trusting in the Lord's mercy; he always awaits us, loves us, has pardoned us with his blood and pardons us every time we go to him to ask his forgiveness. Let us trust in his mercy!

— *Regina Caeli*, Divine Mercy Sunday, April 7, 2013

Reflection: Mary stood by Jesus' side as he suffered and died for you. Implore her to help you understand and receive the love and mercy Jesus has for you.

All Those Who Feel Unloved

We have to remember all those who feel unloved, who have no hope for the future, and who have given up on life out of discouragement, disappointment, or fear. We have to learn to be on the side of the poor, and not just indulge in rhetoric about the poor! Let us go out to meet them, look into their eyes, and listen to them. The poor provide us with a concrete opportunity to encounter Christ himself, and to touch his suffering flesh.

— World Youth Day Message, April 13, 2014

Reflection: In the Gospel of Matthew, Chapter 25, Jesus reminds us that whatever we do to the least, we do to Jesus as well. A personal encounter with the poor gives us a deep encounter with Our Lord and his mercy. We understand how poor we truly are! When is the next time you can encounter the poor? Where can you volunteer?

The Fabric of Society

Jesus' sacrifice on the cross is nothing else than the culmination of the way he lived his entire life. Moved by his example, we want to enter fully into the fabric of society, sharing the lives of all, listening to their concerns, helping them materially and spiritually in their needs, rejoicing with those who rejoice, weeping with those who weep; arm in arm with others, we are committed to building a new world.

— *Evangelii Gaudium*

Reflection: What does living out Jesus' mercy on the cross look like on a practical level each day? How does it change your attitude? Your look? Your smile? Your speech? Ask yourself if you're living in isolation or walking "arm in arm with others."

Keeping the Window Open

God always surprises us! It is God who calls; however, it is important to have a daily relationship with him, to listen to him in silence before the tabernacle and deep within ourselves, to speak with him, to draw near to the sacraments. Having this familiar relationship with the Lord is like keeping the window of our lives open so that he can make us hear his voice and hear what he wants us to do.

— Address, Meeting with Young People,
October 4, 2013

Reflection: Are you open to God's surprises? When you receive the Lord's grace and mercy in the sacraments, do you talk with him? Do you ask to hear his voice? Soften your heart to God's call and be receptive to what he asks.

Must Ring Out Over and Over

The fire of the Spirit is given in the form of tongues and leads us to believe in Jesus Christ who, by his death and resurrection, reveals and communicates to us the Father's infinite mercy. On the lips of the catechist the first proclamation must ring out over and over: "Jesus Christ loves you; he gave his life to save you; and now he is living at your side every day to enlighten, strengthen, and free you."

— *Evangelii Gaudium*

Reflection: If we are to tell others this message about Jesus, we must first believe it ourselves. Jesus Christ loves you; he gave his life to save you; and now he is living at your side every day to enlighten, strengthen, and free you. Do you believe this?

Not to Condemn the World

"God sent his Son into the world, not to condemn the world, but that the world might be saved through him. He who believes in him is not condemned; he who does not believe is condemned already, because he has not believed in the name of the only Son of God" (Jn 3:17-18)....
Thus judgment is pronounced at every moment of life, as it sums up our faith in the salvation which is present and active in Christ, or of our unbelief, whereby we close in upon ourselves. But if we close ourselves to the love of Jesus, we condemn ourselves.

— General Audience, December 11, 2013

Reflection: We don't have to wait for God's mercy. He is waiting for us to turn to him and ask. He does not condemn us; he wants to save us, if we believe. Open yourself up even more to the love of Jesus. Move forward confident of his love for you.

Show Your Almighty Power

[One of the opening prayers at Mass says] something that might go unnoticed.... "Father, you show your almighty power in your mercy and forgiveness."

God's power is so great that it is greater than the power he had to create the world. It is the power to forgive. But in order for him to do so, we need to make room for him. We need to open our hearts so that he can enter with his mercy and forgiveness.

— Homily on the Forty-third Anniversary of the Community of Sant'Egidio, September 24, 2011, *Only Love Can Save Us*

Reflection: It can be so easy to take God's forgiveness for granted. It is a sign of his power that he is able to remove the stain of sin and guilt from our lives, but only if we let him. Pope Francis asks us to make room for God in our lives. What does that mean for you?

Seventy Times Seven

Christ, who told us to forgive one another "seventy times seven" (Mt 18:22), has given us his example: he has forgiven us seventy times seven. Time and time again he bears us on his shoulders. No one can strip us of the dignity bestowed upon us by this boundless and unfailing love.

With a tenderness which never disappoints, but is always capable of restoring our joy, he makes it possible for us to lift up our heads and to start anew. Let us not flee from the resurrection of Jesus, let us never give up, come what will.

— *Evangelii Gaudium*

Reflection: Do you want to be free from grudges? Are you consumed by what others have done to you? The solution is to turn to Jesus' mercy. He has forgiven us, even when we didn't deserve it. He can give you the power to forgive others as well.

Wonderfully Complicated

Jesus wants us to touch human misery, to touch the suffering flesh of others. He hopes that we will stop looking for those personal or communal niches which shelter us from the maelstrom of human misfortune and instead enter into the reality of other people's lives and know the power of tenderness. Whenever we do so, our lives become wonderfully complicated.

— *Evangelii Gaudium*

Reflection: The seven corporal works of mercy are: feed the hungry, give drink to the thirsty, clothe the naked, shelter the homeless, visit the sick, visit the imprisoned, and bury the dead. It's easy to dismiss taking on one of these because they can inconvenience us and make us uncomfortable. But this is what encountering the poor is all about. Are you willing to have your life become wonderfully complicated?

Witness With Joy

We reject him too many times, we prefer to remain closed in our errors and the anxiety of our sins. But Jesus does not desist and never ceases to offer himself and his grace which saves us!...

This is a message of hope, a message of salvation, ancient and ever new. And we are called to witness with joy to this message of the Gospel of life, to the Gospel of light, of hope and of love. For Jesus' message is this: life, light, hope, and love.

— Angelus, January 5, 2014

Reflection: When we remain closed in on ourselves, we often cannot fully receive God's mercy. Consider the ways in which anxiety for your sins and anxiety in general close you in on yourself and block the work of God's mercy in your life. What's one way you can lay aside anxiety this week so that you can be a witness to others?

Forward Without Fear

We must not grow weary, then, of keeping watch over our thoughts and our attitudes, in order that we may be given even now a foretaste of the warmth and splendor of God's face — and this will be beautiful — which in eternal life we shall contemplate in all its fullness.

Forward, thinking of this judgment which begins now, which has already begun. Forward, doing so in such a way that our hearts open to Jesus and to his salvation; forward without fear, for Jesus' love is greater, and if we ask forgiveness for our sins, he will forgive us. This is what Jesus is like. Forward then with this certainty, which will bring us to the glory of heaven!

— General Audience, December 11, 2013

Reflection: Benedictine Abbot Boniface Wimmer once said: "Forward, always forward, everywhere forward! We must not be held back by debts, bad years or by difficulties of the times. Man's adversity is God's opportunity." Where is God asking you to move forward to be more merciful? What is holding you back?

God Prefers the Margins

Starting from Galilee, Jesus teaches us that no one is excluded from the salvation of God, rather it is from the margins that God prefers to begin, from the least, so as to reach everyone. He teaches us a method, his method, which also expresses the content, which is the Father's mercy.

— Angelus, January 26, 2014

Reflection: Jesus' Gospel and his mercy always seem to turn everything upside down. The rich are made lowly while the poor are raised up. The important are insignificant while the least are exalted. In what areas of life does your perspective need to change to reflect God's perspective? How can you see with his eyes?

Indifference

Indifference: human indifference causes the needy so much pain! And worse, the indifference of Christians! On the fringes of society so many men and women are tried by indigence, but also by dissatisfaction with life and by frustration. So many are forced to emigrate from their homeland, risking their lives. Many more, every day, carry the weight of an economic system that exploits human beings, imposing on them an unbearable "yoke," which the few privileged do not want to bear.

To each of these children of the Father in heaven, Jesus repeats, "Come to me, all of you." But he also says it to those who have everything, but whose heart is empty and without God. Even to them, Jesus addresses this invitation, "Come to me." Jesus' invitation is for everyone. But especially for those who suffer the most.

— Angelus, July 6, 2014

Reflection: Where are you indifferent? Where have you lost the ability to love? What can help you wake up from considering only your needs and wants?

As Prodigal Sons

Be brave! Respond to the love of God with enthusiasm, as beloved children; respond with trust when you return to the merciful Father as prodigal sons. Rejoice always for the grace of being children of God, and bring this joy to the world.

— General Audience, June 4, 2014

Reflection: We are able to trust as prodigal sons and daughters because we have experienced God's mercy and continue to be grateful for it. Are you grateful for God's mercy? Do you take it for granted? Gratitude can make a huge difference in your relationship with God.

We Need to Be Saved!

Dear friends, the Gospel does not only concern religion. It concerns man, the whole of man; it concerns the world, society, and human civilization. The Gospel is God's message of salvation for mankind.

When we say "message of salvation," this is not simply a way of speaking, these are not mere words or empty words like so many today. Mankind truly needs to be saved! We see it every day when we flip through newspapers or watch the news on television; but we also see it around us, in people, in situations; and we see it in ourselves! Each one of us needs to be saved! We cannot do it alone! We need to be saved!

— Address, Meeting with Young People,
October 4, 2013

Reflection: Do you believe that you need to be saved? Are you striving to get yourself and everyone you know to heaven? What does it look like to make the message of salvation more of a priority in your life?

A Weak Fragile Sinner

What can I, a weak fragile sinner, do? God says to you: do not be afraid of holiness, do not be afraid to aim high, to let yourself be loved and purified by God, do not be afraid to let yourself be guided by the Holy Spirit. Let us be infected by the holiness of God.... It is the meeting of our weakness with the strength of his grace; it is having faith in his action that allows us to live in charity, to do everything with joy and humility, for the glory of God and as a service to our neighbor.

— General Audience, October 2, 2013

Reflection: Do you have a desire to be a saint? No matter where you are in your spiritual life, open your heart to God's mercy and love. Do not be afraid of your own weaknesses or of what God may ask of you. He strengthens every "weak fragile sinner" who turns to him.

The Quicksand of Sin

"You have heard that it was said, 'You shall love your neighbor and hate your enemy.' But I say to you, love your enemies and pray for those who persecute you" (Mt 5:43-44). Jesus asks those who would follow him to love those who do not deserve it, without expecting anything in return, and in this way to fill the emptiness present in human hearts, relationships, families, communities, and in the entire world....

Christ came to save us, to show us the way, the only way out of the quicksand of sin, and this way of holiness is mercy, that mercy which he has shown, and daily continues to show, to us. To be a saint is not a luxury. It is necessary for the salvation of the world. This is what the Lord is asking of us.

— Homily, February 23, 2014

Reflection: What does it mean that the "way of holiness is mercy"? How is the Lord asking you to follow this path? Where is he leading you?

Running in Vain?

When St. Paul approached the apostles in Jerusalem to discern whether he was "running or had run in vain" (Gal 2:2), the key criterion of authenticity which they presented was that he should not forget the poor (cf. Gal 2:10).... We may not always be able to reflect adequately the beauty of the Gospel, but there is one sign which we should never lack: the option for those who are least, those whom society discards.

— *Evangelii Gaudium*

Reflection: What does it mean to have an option for the least? How would your life be different if you preferred to serve the least first?

We Are All Poor

A pilgrim is a person who makes himself poor and sets forth on a journey.... We can never think ourselves self-sufficient, masters of our own lives. We cannot be content with remaining withdrawn, secure in our convictions.

Before the mystery of God we are all poor. We realize that we must constantly be prepared to go out from ourselves, docile to God's call and open to the future that he wishes to create for us.

— Address, Pilgrimage to the Holy Land,
May 25, 2014

Reflection: We are all pilgrims on a journey toward the future. Travel always brings the unexpected, but if we are docile to God's call, we need not fear. Where are you on your journey of life? Are you relying on God's mercy? Stumbling? Tentative about the next step? Ask the Holy Spirit to lead you.

The Grace to Be Disciples and Missionaries

And this is what baptism works in us: it gives us grace and hands on the faith to us.... Everyone: the littlest one is also a missionary; and the one who seems to be the greatest is a disciple.

But one of you might say, "Bishops are not disciples, bishops know everything; the pope knows everything, he is not a disciple." No, the bishops and the pope must also be disciples, because if they are not disciples, they do no good. They cannot be missionaries; they cannot transmit the faith. We must all be disciples and missionaries.

— General Audience, January 15, 2014

Reflection: We must respond to the grace and mercy received at our baptism by being missionary disciples. In what ways are you a disciple and a missionary? Where can you improve? What is God calling you to do?

Serene Happiness

Let us ask Our Lady to give us the grace to endure with patience and to overcome with love. How many people — so many old people — have taken this path! And it is beautiful to see them: they have that beautiful countenance, that serene happiness. They do not say much, but have a patient heart, a heart filled with love. They know what forgiving enemies means, they know what it is to pray for enemies. So many Christians are like that!

— Homily, *Domus Sanctae Marthae*, May 24, 2013

Reflection: Do you have a patient heart? Are you able to overcome with love and a serene happiness? Examine your life and find one area where you need to overcome difficulties with patience. Ask God for the grace to be merciful.

In the Midst of Darkness

The joy of the Gospel is such that it cannot be taken away from us by anyone or anything (cf. Jn 16:22). The evils of our world — and those of the Church — must not be excuses for diminishing our commitment and our fervor. Let us look upon them as challenges which can help us to grow. With the eyes of faith, we can see the light which the Holy Spirit always radiates in the midst of darkness, never forgetting that "where sin increased, grace has abounded all the more" (Rom 5:20).

— *Evangelii Gaudium*

Reflection: Light shines brighter in darkness. Jesus said, "Let your light so shine before men, that they may see your good works and give glory to your Father who is in heaven" (Mt. 5:16). Ask the Holy Spirit to help you be a light this week at home, at your parish, in your workplace, and in your neighborhood.

Living With Joy

And so, let us ask ourselves: How is it possible to live the joy which comes from faith, in the family, today? But I ask you also: Is it possible to live this joy, or is it not possible? A saying of Jesus in the Gospel of Matthew speaks to us: "Come to me, all who labor and are heavy laden, and I will give you rest" (11:28).

— Address, Pilgrimage of Families, October 26, 2013

Reflection: To live with joy and to give joy to others is a great act of mercy. Who needs your joy today? Turn to the Lord to recharge your joy in him.

Ultimate Thanksgiving

Jesus' gesture at the Last Supper is the ultimate thanksgiving to the Father for his love, for his mercy. "Thanksgiving," in Greek, is expressed as "eucharist." And that is why the Sacrament is called the Eucharist: it is the supreme thanksgiving to the Father, who so loved us that he gave us his Son out of love. This is why the term Eucharist includes the whole of that act, which is the act of God and man together, the act of Jesus Christ, true God and true Man.

— General Audience, February 5, 2014

Reflection: In the Eucharist, we are able to encounter God's mercy in the flesh. Right now, thank God for this great gift. Ask him to open your heart wider to receive the Eucharist with a more grateful heart.

Recognize the Suffering Christ

Jesus, the evangelizer par excellence and the Gospel in person, identifies especially with the little ones (cf. Mt 25:40)…. It is essential to draw near to new forms of poverty and vulnerability, in which we are called to recognize the suffering Christ, even if this appears to bring us no tangible and immediate benefits. I think of the homeless, the addicted, refugees, indigenous peoples, the elderly who are increasingly isolated and abandoned, and many others.

— *Evangelii Gaudium*

Reflection: We can often dismiss the poor because we don't think our actions will change anything. We so often want to help only if we know we are making a difference. What ways can you give without expectations of success?

On a Pilgrimage

On the First Sunday of Advent, we begin a new liturgical year; that is, a new journey of the People of God with Jesus Christ, our Shepherd, who guides us through history toward the fulfillment of the kingdom of God. But where are we journeying? Is there a common goal? And what is this goal? . . .

[Jesus] is both guide and goal of our pilgrimage, of the pilgrimage of the entire People of God; and in his light the other peoples may also walk toward the kingdom of justice, toward the kingdom of peace.

— Angelus, December 1, 2013

Reflection: This Advent, go on a pilgrimage with Jesus. Ask Jesus to help you make goals and to be your guide. How often will you pray? What practical steps will you take? Build the kingdom of justice with him.

In Humility He Revealed Himself

The story of Naaman, the commander of the army of the king of Aram, is remarkable. In order to be healed of leprosy, he turns to the prophet of God, Elisha, who does not perform magic or demand anything unusual of him, but asks him simply to trust in God and to wash in the waters of the river. Not, however, in one of the great rivers of Damascus, but in the little stream of the Jordan. Naaman is left surprised, even taken aback. What kind of God is this who asks for something so simple? He wants to turn back, but then he goes ahead, he immerses himself in the Jordan, and is immediately healed (cf. 2 Kg 5:1-4).

There it is: God surprises us. It is precisely in poverty, in weakness, and in humility that he reveals himself and grants us his love, which saves us, heals us, and gives us strength. He asks us only to obey his word and to trust in him.

— Homily, October 13, 2013

Reflection: The Lord is calling you to trust in his mercy for healing in your life. Where in your life do you need this the most? How will you respond to his healing touch this week?

Do You Really Want to Be Happy?

Tell me: Do you really want to be happy? . . . If you are really open to the deepest aspirations of your hearts, you will realize that you possess an unquenchable thirst for happiness, and this will allow you to expose and reject the "low cost" offers and approaches all around you.

When we look only for success, pleasure, and possessions, and we turn these into idols, we may well have moments of exhilaration, an illusory sense of satisfaction, but ultimately we become enslaved, never satisfied, always looking for more.

— World Youth Day Message, April 13, 2014

Reflection: What "low cost" offers do you accept instead of God's mercy? What idols stand in our way? Do you want to be happy? Find ways to choose God over easy solutions. Don't be afraid to make a radical decision to make this possible.

Confident Abandonment

A person tends to die as he has lived. If my life has been a journey with the Lord, a journey of trust in his immense mercy, I will be prepared to accept the final moment of my earthly life as the definitive, confident abandonment into his welcoming hands, awaiting the face-to-face contemplation of his face.

— General Audience, November 27, 2013

Reflection: Is your life a journey with the Lord? Do you sometimes leave him behind? When in your life do you do this and why? No matter where you are in your journey with God, abandon yourself to his mercy and resolve to follow him more closely.

Do We Pray for the Church?

Do we pray for the Church? For the whole Church?... It is easy for us to pray when we have need of something, or to thank the Lord for something we have been given. [But we don't always remember] to pray for the Church, for those we do not know but who are our brothers and sisters because they have received the same baptism, and to say to the Lord, "They are yours, they are ours, protect them."

— Homily, *Domus Sanctae Marthae*, April 30, 2013

Reflection: To pray for others is a great act of mercy. When we do, we remove ourselves from the center of attention and put others first. Who needs prayer right now in the world? Pray on behalf of those who come to mind.

Impossible to Persevere

It is impossible to persevere in a fervent evangelization unless we are convinced from personal experience that it is not the same thing to have known Jesus as not to have known him, not the same thing to walk with him as to walk blindly, not the same thing to hear his word as not to know it, and not the same thing to contemplate him, to worship him, to find our peace in him, as not to.

It is not the same thing to try to build the world with his Gospel as to try to do so by our own lights.

— *Evangelii Gaudium*

Reflection: Is your life different because of Jesus? How and to what extent? In what ways do you need to change in order to walk more closely with him? What priorities do you need to rearrange?

Become Small

If God, in the Christmas mystery, reveals himself not as One who remains on high and dominates the universe, but as the One who bends down, descends to the little and poor earth, it means that, to be like him, we should not put ourselves above others, but indeed lower ourselves, place ourselves at the service of others, become small with the small and poor with the poor.

It is regrettable to see a Christian who does not want to lower himself, who does not want to serve. A Christian who struts about is ugly: this is not Christian, it is pagan. The Christian serves, he lowers himself.

— General Audience, December 18, 2013

Reflection: The attitude of mercy is an attitude of service. During the Advent and Christmas season, we can easily fall into the mindset of: What's in it for me? How can you continue to serve others this season in all things?

Room for All Men and Women

As far as faith, the hinge of the Christian life, is concerned, the Mother of God shared our condition.... Our pilgrimage of faith has been inseparably linked to Mary ever since Jesus, dying on the cross, gave her to us as our mother, saying: "Behold your mother!" (Jn 19:27).

These words serve as a testament, bequeathing to the world a mother. From that moment on, the Mother of God also became our mother!... Her sorrowing heart was enlarged to make room for all men and women, all, whether good or bad, and she loves them as she loved Jesus.

— Homily, January 1, 2014

Reflection: In the hour of his death, the hour of his greatest mercy, Jesus gave us Mary to be our mother. What role does Mary play in your life? Is she important? Are you indifferent? Do you need to learn more about her? Mary wants to be your mother. She wants to help you know and love Jesus more. Open up your life to her even in a small way.

The Face of the Needy, the Face of Jesus

Thanks to baptism, we are capable of forgiving and of loving even those who offend us and do evil to us. By our baptism, we recognize in the least and in the poor the face of the Lord who visits us and makes himself close. Baptism helps us to recognize in the face of the needy, the suffering, and also of our neighbor, the face of Jesus. All this is possible thanks to the power of baptism!

— General Audience, January 8, 2014

Reflection: At first, it may seem that our baptism has little to do with helping the needy. But baptism is a beautiful reflection of God's mercy for us. Many of us were helpless infants during our baptism. We had done nothing and could do nothing, and yet, in our baptism, God gave us his mercy. Let's live out this baptism by giving God's mercy to those in need.

Proclaiming the Name of Jesus

The Church's roots are in the teaching of the apostles, the authentic witnesses of Christ, but she looks to the future, she has the firm consciousness of being sent — sent by Jesus — of being missionary, bearing the name of Jesus by her prayer, proclaiming it, and testifying to it.

A Church that is closed in on herself and in the past, a Church that only sees the little rules of behavior, of attitude, is a Church that betrays her own identity; a closed Church betrays her own identity!

— General Audience, October 16, 2013

Reflection: The spiritual works of mercy call us to admonish the sinner and instruct the ignorant. In our society today, doing these things can come off as intolerant. How are these actions actually merciful? What can help you practice them when appropriate?

Encounter the Mercy of God

The Church enables us to encounter the mercy of God which transforms us, for in her Jesus Christ is present, who has given her the true confession of faith, the fullness of the sacramental life, and the authenticity of the ordained ministry. In the Church, each one of us finds what is needed to believe, to live as Christians, to become holy and to journey to every place and through every age.

— General Audience, October 9, 2013

Reflection: What's your relationship with the Church like? The Church is a vessel of God's mercy here on earth. Try to become more involved in your parish this next month.

I Will Give You Rest

"Come to me, all who labor and are heavy laden, and I will give you rest" (Mt 11:28). When Jesus says this, he has before him the people he meets every day on the streets of Galilee: very many simple people, the poor, the sick, sinners, those who are marginalized.... These people always followed him to hear his word — a word that gave hope! Jesus' words always give hope!

— Angelus, July 6, 2014

Reflection: What helps you see beyond your current situation or your moments of suffering? God's mercy is always trying to find you. It's always trying to reach you. Be open to allowing him to meet you. Let him give you hope.

We Feel at Peace

[Forgiveness] reminds us that we can truly be at peace only if we allow ourselves to be reconciled, in the Lord Jesus, with the Father and with the brethren. And we have all felt this in our hearts, when we have gone to confession with a soul weighed down and with a little sadness; and when we receive Jesus' forgiveness, we feel at peace, with that peace of soul which is so beautiful, and which only Jesus can give, only him.

— General Audience, February 19, 2014

Reflection: Do you want true peace? Examine your life. Where have you sinned against God? Where have you sinned against others? Turn to the Lord for forgiveness. He can give the inner peace that you are looking for.

The Virgin of Guadalupe

When the image of the Virgin appeared on the tilma of Juan Diego, it was the prophecy of an embrace: Mary's embrace of all the peoples of the vast expanses of America — the peoples who already lived there, and those who were yet to come.

Mary's embrace showed what America — North and South — is called to be: a land where different peoples come together; a land prepared to accept human life at every stage, from the mother's womb to old age; a land which welcomes immigrants, and the poor and the marginalized, in every age. A land of generosity.

— General Audience, December 11, 2013

Reflection: Mary's appearance in Mexico was a great act of mercy and a wonderful symbol of God's embrace. How can you live out Mary's embrace, especially in relation to immigrants? What practical step can you take to learn more about the Church's teaching regarding the care of immigrants, the poor, and the marginalized?

The Greatness of His Mercy

The Third Sunday of Advent ... is called Gaudete Sunday; that is, the Sunday of joy....

God is he who comes to save us and who seeks to help, especially those who are fearful of heart.... We are invited to strengthen the weak hands, to make firm the feeble knees, to be strong and to fear not, because our God always shows us the greatness of his mercy. He gives us the strength to go forward.

— Angelus, December 15, 2013

Reflection: If we want to see the greatness of God's mercy, then we need to be bold enough to open our lives and weaknesses to him each day. Pray for the courage to do so!

It's an Awful Sign!

The care given to the elderly, like that of children, is an indicator of the quality of a community. When the elderly are tossed aside, when the elderly are isolated and sometimes fade away due to a lack of care, it's an awful sign! How nice instead is that alliance between young and old ... where everyone gives and receives!

— Address to the Sant'Egidio Community, June 15, 2014

Reflection: When is the last time that you visited a nursing home? There are so many elderly who don't receive visits from anyone. Take time this Sunday to visit, even for just a few minutes. Teach others about this great act of mercy by taking someone with you.

Wishes No One to Be Lost

Christ embraces all of humanity and wishes no one to be lost. "For God sent the Son into the world, not to condemn the world, but that the world might be saved through him" (Jn 3:17). He does it without oppressing or constraining anyone to open to him the doors of heart and mind. . . .

Every activity therefore must be distinguished by an attitude of service to persons, especially those furthest away and less known. Service is the soul of that fraternity that builds up peace.

— World Day of Peace Message, January 1, 2014

Reflection: Who have you condemned? Who do you ignore? Humans can be quick to dismiss others, but God continues to offer his mercy to everyone. How can you take on the mercy of God? Who do you need to serve?

Your First Job

Prayer is the first job of your community, and it consists in listening to the Word of God — this bread, the bread that gives us strength, that lets us go forward — but also in turning our eyes to him: "Look to him, and be radiant; so your faces shall never be ashamed," says the Psalm (34:5). He who sees the Lord, sees others.

— Address to the Sant'Egidio Community, June 15, 2014

Reflection: Does your prayer life increase your ability to see others? If you want to reach others, do you pray for the ability to do so?

Cloaked in the Mercy and Love of God

Dear friends, Psalm 34 tells us to pray like this: "This poor man cried, and the Lord heard him, and saved him out of all his troubles. The angel of the Lord encamps around those who fear him, and delivers them" (vv. 6-7). Let us ask the Lord for the grace to unite our voice to that of the poor, to welcome the gift of fear of the Lord, and to be able to recognize ourselves, together with them, as cloaked in the mercy and love of God, who is our Father, our dad.

— General Audience, June 11, 2014

Reflection: Read Psalm 34. Using Pope Francis' words for your meditation, what is God saying to you? What should you do as a result?

A Courageous Prayer

Miracles happen. But they need prayer! A courageous prayer, that struggles for that miracle. Not like those prayers of courtesy: Ah, I will pray for you! Followed by one Our Father, a Hail Mary, and then I forget. No! It takes a brave prayer like that of Abraham who was struggling with the Lord to save the city, like that of Moses who prayed, his hands held high when he grew weary.

— Homily, *Domus Sanctae Marthae*, May 20, 2013

Reflection: Is your prayer brave? Is it courageous? Are you confident that courageous prayer can work miracles? Pray for others with confidence.

Change My Heart

"Well! Father, I am a sinner, I have tremendous sins, how can I possibly feel part of the Church?" Dear brother, dear sister, this is exactly what the Lord wants, that you say to him: "Lord, here I am, with my sins." Is one of you here without sin? Anyone? No one; not one of us. We all carry our sins with us. But the Lord wants to hear us say to him: "Forgive me, help me to walk, change my heart!" And the Lord can change your heart.

— General Audience, October 2, 2013

Reflection: Do you believe that the Lord can change your heart? Think of what you struggle with the most. Offer this to God. He is waiting for you. Pray to him: "Forgive me, help me to walk, change my heart."

The Definitive Word

How much pain and desperation are caused by self-centeredness which gradually takes the form of envy, selfishness, competition, and the thirst for power and money! At times, it seems that these realities are destined to have the upper hand.

Christmas, on the other hand, inspires in us Christians the certainty that the final, definitive word belongs to the Prince of Peace, who changes "swords into plowshares and spears into pruning hooks" (cf. Is 2:4), transforming selfishness into self-giving and revenge into forgiveness....

Christians are called to give witness to God's love and mercy. We must never cease to do good, even when it is difficult and demanding.

— Address, January 13, 2014

Reflection: Jesus' coming radically changes the world. Most important, this act of mercy is supposed to change our hearts. Where is it difficult and demanding for you to do good right now? Is it with a co-worker? Is it in a relationship with a relative? How can you witness to God's love in these situations?

In the Face of Our Neighbor

Whoever has fed, welcomed, visited, loved one of the least and poorest of men, will have done it to the Son of God. Let us entrust ourselves to the maternal intercession of Mary, the Mother of Jesus and our mother, that she may help us this holy Christmastide, which is already close at hand, to see in the face of our neighbor, especially the weakest and most marginalized people, the image of the Son of God made man.

— General Audience, December 18, 2013

Reflection: Who are the weak among you? Who are the marginalized? We should certainly help the poor, especially in this season, but there may be others around us who need our help as well. Are there people in your parish, neighborhood, or family you could reach out to? How could you treat them like Jesus?

The Kingdom of God

Reading the Scriptures also makes it clear that the Gospel is not merely about our personal relationship with God. Nor should our loving response to God be seen simply as an accumulation of small personal gestures to individuals in need, a kind of "charity à la carte," or a series of acts aimed solely at easing our conscience.

The Gospel is about the kingdom of God (cf. Lk 4:43); it is about loving God who reigns in our world. To the extent that he reigns within us, the life of society will be a setting for universal fraternity, justice, peace, and dignity.

— *Evangelii Gaudium*

Reflection: Over what part of your life does God still need to reign? What area of your life do you still try to control? Where do you hold back because you are afraid of having God in charge? Turn to his mercy to give you the grace to make him the Lord of everything.

Love and Adore Him

Above all else, this is what Christmas bids us to do: give glory to God, for he is good, he is faithful, he is merciful. Today I voice my hope that everyone will come to know the true face of God, the Father who has given us Jesus. My hope is that everyone will feel God's closeness, live in his presence, love him and adore him.

— *Urbi et Orbi*, December 25, 2013

Reflection: Christmas is a busy season. We can get caught up in the presents, the decorations, and all the events and parties. Take some time to pray in gratitude to God. Tell him all the things you are thankful for. Especially tell him how thankful you are for the gift of his mercy in sending his Son into the world.

Do Not Be Afraid

CHRISTMAS EVE

On this night, let us share the joy of the Gospel: God loves us, he so loves us that he gave us his Son to be our brother, to be light in our darkness. To us the Lord repeats: "Do not be afraid!" (Lk 2:10). As the angels said to the shepherds: "Do not be afraid!" And I also repeat to all of you: Do not be afraid!

Our Father is patient, he loves us, he gives us Jesus to guide us on the way which leads to the promised land. Jesus is the light who brightens the darkness. He is mercy: our Father always forgives us. He is our peace.

— Homily, December 24, 2013

Reflection: When you are fearful, where do you turn? What brings you peace? Take the fears you have right now and give them to God. Practice turning to God throughout the day when life causes you to worry and fear.

He Has Shared Our Journey

CHRISTMAS

[Jesus] has entered our history; he has shared our journey. He came to free us from darkness and to grant us light. In him was revealed the grace, the mercy, and the tender love of the Father: Jesus is Love incarnate. He is not simply a teacher of wisdom, he is not an ideal for which we strive while knowing that we are hopelessly distant from it. He is the meaning of life and history, who has pitched his tent in our midst.

— Homily, December 24, 2013

Reflection: Because God became man, he has endured the struggles, fears, and questions that we endure. He has experienced pain as we've experienced pain. He has shared our journey. This knowledge can help us receive his mercy with gratitude, knowing that Jesus also looked to the mercy of his Father. Think about the meaning of Christmas and let it give you inspiration and hope for the future.

A Dawn of New Life

The feast of St. Stephen is in full harmony with the deeper meaning of Christmas. In martyrdom, in fact, violence is conquered by love, death by life. The Church sees in the sacrifice of the martyrs their "birth into heaven." Therefore, today we celebrate the "birth" of Stephen, which in its depths springs from the birth of Christ. Jesus transforms the death of those who love him into a dawn of new life!

— Angelus, December 26, 2013

Reflection: What death, sin, pain, or suffering do you see around you? How can you live out the deeper meaning of Christmas in these situations?

In Search of Security

Almost every day the television and papers carry news of refugees fleeing from hunger, war, and other grave dangers, in search of security and a dignified life for themselves and for their families....

Therefore, as we fix our gaze on the Holy Family of Nazareth as they were forced to become refugees, let us think of the tragedy of those migrants and refugees who are victims of rejection and exploitation, who are victims of human trafficking and of slave labor.

— Angelus, December 29, 2013

Reflection: The corporal works of mercy instruct us to help the homeless and the imprisoned. Pope Francis speaks of many modern forms of slavery in our world today — people who are held in bondage in some way and who don't have a real home. Pray for these people, but also explore ways that you can help relieve their suffering.

Are We Like Herod?

FEAST OF THE HOLY INNOCENTS

And we have to ask ourselves: Who are we, as we stand before the Child Jesus? Who are we, standing as we stand before today's children? Are we like Mary and Joseph, who welcomed Jesus and cared for him with the love of a father and a mother? Or are we like Herod, who wanted to eliminate him? Are we like the shepherds, who went in haste to kneel before him in worship and offer him their humble gifts? Or are we indifferent?

— Homily, May 25, 2014

Reflection: During this season, we are called to invite the Child Jesus more deeply into our hearts. Imagine the scene of the Nativity or take a look at a Nativity set. Ponder the Child Jesus. Who are you before him? What can you do to welcome him? Who are you before today's children? What more can you do to be more merciful?

Jesus Is God-with-us

The presence of God among men did not take place in a perfect, idyllic world but rather in this real world, which is marked by so many things both good and bad, by division, wickedness, poverty, arrogance, and war.

He chose to live in our history as it is, with all the weight of its limitations and of its tragedies. In doing so, he has demonstrated in an unequaled manner his merciful and truly loving disposition toward the human creature. He is God-with-us. Jesus is God-with-us. Do you believe this?

— General Audience, December 18, 2013

Reflection: Mother Teresa was reportedly inspired by a poem that states, in part: "People are often unreasonable, irrational, and self-centered. Forgive them anyway." Christmas is a reminder of God's plan to enter into our brokenness and to be merciful anyway. What part of your brokenness does God need to enter into? He is with you. Don't hide your brokenness from him.

Indestructible Love

With the birth of Jesus the heavens open! God gives us in Christ the guarantee of an indestructible love.... And it is possible for each one of us, if we allow ourselves to be suffused with God's love, which is given to us for the first time in baptism by means of the Holy Spirit. Let us allow ourselves to be invaded by God's love! This is the great time of mercy! Do not forget it: this is the great time of mercy!

— Angelus, January 12, 2014

Reflection: Giving ourselves to others in love takes courage. We can only do this knowing that we possess God's indestructible love. Ask the Holy Spirit to help you be invaded by God's love so that you can give it to others.

Let Us Courageously Ask

As [the year] draws to a close, we gather up, as in a basket, the days, weeks, and months we have lived in order to offer them all to the Lord. And let us courageously ask ourselves: How have we lived the time which he has given us? Have we used it primarily for ourselves, for our own interests, or have we also sought to spend it on others? How much time have we reserved for being with God in prayer, in silence, in adoration?

— Homily, December 31, 2013

Reflection: Each season and moment in our lives is a gift from God. When we reflect back it is a chance to reflect with gratitude on God's mercy, love, and providence in our lives. What have you done with these gifts? Where can you improve? Make a resolution to make a change toward greater freedom and mercy this next year.

Index

About the Editor

Kevin Cotter is a missionary with FOCUS (the Fellowship of Catholic University Students), where he serves as the Director of Curriculum and Web. As the creator of PopeAlarm.com, Kevin notified over one hundred thousand people about Pope Francis' election via text and e-mail. He holds an M.A. in Sacred Scripture from the Augustine Institute and lives in Denver, Colorado, with his wife, Lisa, and their young children. Kevin dedicates his work on this book to his parents, Bob and Laura Cotter: "In gratitude for all of the love and mercy you have shown me."